# Winnicott and Pa

Whitehead's Paradox

# Winnicott and Paradox
*from birth to creation*

Anne Clancier and Jeannine Kalmanovitch

*Translated from the French by Alan Sheridan*

FOREWORD BY PRINCE MASUD KHAN

TAVISTOCK PUBLICATIONS
London and New York

First published as *Le Paradoxe de Winnicott* by
Les Editions Payot
© 1984 Payot, Paris
English translation
First published in 1987 by
Tavistock Publications Ltd
11 New Fetter Lane, London EC4P 4EE

Published in the USA by
Tavistock Publications
in association with Methuen, Inc.
29 West 35th Street, New York NY 10001

© 1987 Alan Sheridan
Preface © 1984 Simone Decobert
Foreword © 1987 Prince Masud Khan

Photoset by Rowland Phototypesetting Ltd
Bury St Edmunds, Suffolk
Printed in Great Britain at the
University Press, Cambridge

*British Library Cataloguing in Publication Data*
Clancier, Anne
    Winnicott and paradox: from birth to creation.
    1. Winnicott, D. W.    2. Child psychology
    I. Title    II. Kalmanovitch, Jeannine
    III. Le paradoxe de Winnicott, *English*
    155.4′092′4        BF721

    ISBN 0-422-60370-8
    ISBN 0-422-60380-5 Pbk

*Library of Congress Cataloging in Publication Data*
Clancier, Anne.
    Winnicott and paradox.

    Translation of: Le paradoxe de Winnicott.
    Bibliography: p.
    Includes index.
    1. Child analysis.    2. Winnicott,
    D. W. (Donald Woods), 1896–1971.
    I. Kalmanovitch, Jeannine.    II. Title.
    RJ504.2.C5713 1987        618.92′8917        87-492
    ISBN 0-422-60370-8
    ISBN 0-422-60380-5 (pbk.)

*To* Donald W. Winnicott, *so living in our memory*

*To* Clare Winnicott, *who shared her dream with us, with our gratitude*

# Contents

# Illustrations

# The authors

Anne Clancier, physician, psychoanalyst, and author of psychoanalytic work on art and literature, has long experience of therapy with both adults and children.

Jeannine Kalmanovitch, the translator of most of Winnicott's work into French and a close friend of his.

# Acknowledgements

We would like to thank:

Joyce Coles, who has generously placed at our disposal photographs and Christmas cards designed by D. W. Winnicott over the years. Not all of this material has been reproduced here, but we have drawn extensively on the memories of a woman who was his secretary for over twenty years.

Thérèse Albenque, librarian of the Institut de Psychanalyse, who, in the most friendly and competent manner, assisted us in our bibliographical research.

The authors and publishers would like to thank the following for their kind permission to reproduce copyright material: The Winnicott Trust for the figure *Frustrated Sculpture*; Chatto & Windus: The Hogarth Press and Basic Books, New York, for figures and text from *Through Paediatrics to Psychoanalysis* by D. W. Winnicott. Copyright © 1975 by the Hogarth Press.

# Preface

A jack-in-the-box. That was how D. W. Winnicott struck me at the Copenhagen Congress in 1959 as I entered a room in which a subcommittee devoted to child analysis was meeting. Sitting on the back row of the room, flattened against it like some disjointed marionette, in an attitude that could not have been more different from that of the dignified chairman that he had adopted a quarter of an hour earlier, during a session devoted to psychotic object relations, or a little earlier when solemnly appointed by the executive committee of the International Psychoanalytical Association as a member of its appointments committee, D. W. Winnicott unwound like a spring and brought back to life an audience that would have been on the verge of slumbering through a debate on 'fantasy and inner reality'. He then gave a brilliant exposition of part of what, in 1960, was to become his famous report on the theory of the parent–infant relationship.

Although I had arrived at the congress with some of the preconceived notions that were then circulating in Paris about Winnicott's work, very little of which had yet been translated, I immediately realized how simplistic they were solely through the presence, the evident depth of thought – the humour and charm, too – in other words, the human quality of the man himself. He had to explain his ideas, almost defend them. This he did with the greatest of ease, for he possessed that self-confidence that characterizes certain discoverers, who are convinced that they have nothing to lose by expounding their observations and hypotheses in all honesty; he also possessed that other kind of self-confidence, which, as Freud said, characterizes the child who knows that he was his parents' favourite, especially his mother's favourite.

On that occasion, the delicate issue was the introduction of the parameter of external reality into treatment, an approach that seemed quite the reverse of the classic psychoanalytical attitude, in which the drives, affects, conflicts, the constitution of the object relation are primary and not secondary. Would he have to find a new conception of the psychical apparatus? Would he have to admit that a gap might exist between the functioning of the infant experiencing his life with the help of his mother's presence and the organization of the drives or of the psyche–soma complex. We were not at the time as used as we are today to authors who are concerned with the level of the non-integrated, who explore and use in primary narcissism the nuclei of the self or the bound nuclei of the pre-ego, such as Winnicott, following in the footsteps of E. Glover or V. Tausk, and followed later by J. Bleger, W. R. Bion, or D. Meltzer. These authors define and conceive original undifferentiation not in the absolute as a state of undifferentiation, but already as a sort of organization that still embraces both the subject and his environment. We know that this datum concerning the original bound nucleus allows a family therapist like A. Ruffiot to propose the hypothesis of a concomitance between the mother–child undifferentiation and the child–group undifferentiation. He then supports Freud's conception according to which a continuity exists between the individual psyche and the collective psyche (*Group Psychology and the Analysis of the Ego*, 1921) and various contemporary researchers are concerned to return to this hypothesis, which Freud regarded as insufficiently developed.

Another explanation for our reticence with regard to D. W. Winnicott's theories concerned what are called his borrowings from the behaviourists. For example, the notion of holding (of the infant), the definition of which is nevertheless quite clear in the article already mentioned:

'The term "holding" is used here to denote not only the actual physical holding of the infant, but also the total environmental provision prior to the concept of *living with*. In other words, it refers to a three-dimensional or space relationship with time gradually added. This overlaps with, but is initiated prior to, instinctual experiences, that in time would determine object relationships.'[1]

These terms, which have led to confusion with similar behaviourist concepts, are nevertheless the first stage in what is to be a strictly psychoanalytical exploration of such a conception. What is even more specific to 'holding' is the notion of dependence. During the holding phase, the child is dependent to a very high degree: he has no way of recognizing maternal care or of controlling it as good or bad; he has to learn to acknowledge his need of maternal care and to link it to his own impulses. He must then find a way of doing without care by hallucinating or building up memories of maternal care, by projecting his own needs and introjecting particular memories of care as he develops his confidence in the environment. And here we come back to the dynamics proper to the experience of non-integration.

This first awareness of the need for care will reappear in the transference during analytical treatment. Thus the role of the analyst will be to respond to it, at the level at which the demand is formulated and with the help of 'ordinary people', the mother, friends, rather than specialized staff. It is true that this constitutes a variation of the classic technique.

A work that had widespread influence on child analysts in France is *Therapeutic Consultations in Child Psychiatry*. It dates from 1971. It defines the minimum of help that is useful and contra-indicates uncontrolled intervention in the family, which, as long as its mental state allows it (and it allows it to go very far), remains the privileged locus in which must take place 'organized regression' in emotional development, movements backwards that are capable of moving the familial dynamics forward, providing they are practised in the presence of a third party, namely, the child psychoanalyst. As we know, D. W. Winnicott was above all a paediatrician, convinced as he was of the need to be trained in that specialization if one is to practise child psychiatry or even the psychiatry of adults. He has been criticized – for example, for the article called 'Hate in the Counter-transference' (1947)[2] – for using a type of reassuring popularization in order to calm the fear of psychoanalysis felt by rejecting mothers, who overcompensate their guilt with excessive care. His use of humour led him to list seventeen good reasons why a mother might hate her child 'even if it's a boy'!

In fact, a more widespread reaction to D. W. Winnicott's writings concerns the question of the variations in technique, a criticism that is inevitably levelled at all those who are concerned with other cases than the classical neuroses. Borderline cases and psychotics do not, like the neurotics, come into analysis at their own request, since what they lack is precisely what Winnicott calls the 'primary environment' and it is this that the analyst must try to provide. In the article, 'Dreaming, Fantasying and Living', the author describes very well 'what it is to feel alive'[3] and we all know how successful his notions of the transitional object and transitional space have been in their relationship to the 'capacity to be alone'. A sense of being alive was precisely what D. W. Winnicott's patients tended to lack.

This book, written by a profoundly Winnicottian team, but a very objective one, takes up the highly original notions of this creative psychoanalyst and stresses their new heuristic dimension – especially by distinguishing it from that of Melanie Klein, whom he respected, but whom he also criticized in an unaggressive manner. We know that he developed the Kleinian notions of precocity, showing that what is deep is not necessarily archaic and that he was interested in the 'primary' human condition proceeding from an undifferentiated chaotic state, prior to the constitution of the psychical structure and therefore to fantasy and the primary object relations, which, for Melanie Klein, were given from the outset. Similarly, he used, but criticized, the direct observation of the newborn infant and of the mother–child interaction so fashionable today, by drawing attention to the fact that the totality of experience is no more perceptible to the observer than the totality of an iceberg.

The greatest lesson to be derived from this inimitable noncon-formist of genius is the need to remain a useful practitioner by approaching the patient in a friendly way, while continuing to improve, outside the session, the indispensable metapsycho-logical constructions, without ever letting the patient perceive anything but empathy, deriving directly from the mother's care for her infant.

*Simone Decobert*
*Director, Institut Claparède*

# Foreword

Donald Winnicott was a curiously peculiar and particular person. The youngest child and only son of Sir George Winnicott, Mayor of Plymouth, he grew up much loved and pampered by his parents and two elder sisters. If he was loved much, much was also expected of him. So paradox, as he was to call it himself, started from the beginning of his life, in his living, in very many ways. Winnicott was a very brilliant student at school and a good athlete. He damaged his hip somehow and there are various versions as to how it happened. He insisted on serving in the Army so during the First World War he became an orderly with the St John's Ambulance Service. After the war he returned to study medicine and from there began the career of the devoted Winnicott to the ordinary devoted mother and her baby.

Life also had been a paradox for Winnicott. He had the best of it and a lot of hurt as well. His first wife, a beautiful operatic singer, went mad, and taking care of her took all his youth. But during that time he did establish himself as a clinician in psychotherapy with children.

When I met Winnicott in 1949 at Paddington Green Clinic, he was amidst five children. All drawing, or what he would call doodling, with him, plus their parents. Winnicott would move from child to child, then go to the parents of the particular child, talk with them and come back, and so on. I witnessed this for two hours. At the end of it he came over to me and said: 'You are Masud Khan?' I said. 'Yes, sir.' He asked me. 'What are you doing here, you are too well dressed to be here?' I was only 25 years of age and a candidate at the British Institute of Psycho-Analysis, but I wasn't going to be taunted by him, so I replied: 'One dresses to the manner born!' Winnicott smiled and said: 'You have some cheek.' From that day a relationship started that was to last till the end of his life in 1971. Winnicott was my supervising analyst for a child case, then my analyst for ten years, then he analysed my wife Svetlana Beriozova. He loved music, she *danced* it. During all this time, since 1949, he asked me to edit his works. Every paper by Winnicott from 1950 to 1970, and every book by Winnicott has been edited by me.

Winnicott was not an easy person to relate to; yet he was a joyous person to be with. The last thing that Winnicott would have wanted was for us to make a myth about him. I have been asked to write a preface to the book by Dr Anne Clancier and Jeannine Kalmanovitch. I can truly recommend this book to any reader who is interested to have some sort of a guide to Winnicott.

Lastly, Winnicott never wrote dogmatically nor did he want to found a school like Melanie Klein, Heinz Hartmann, Anna Freud, and others. He was an Englishman, born to be uniquely himself, without compelling his style of work or sensibility on anyone. The paradox that haunted D.W.W, as we call him, was that living and dying were of the same fabric made.

Prince Masud Khan M.A.,D.LITT.
29 August, 1986

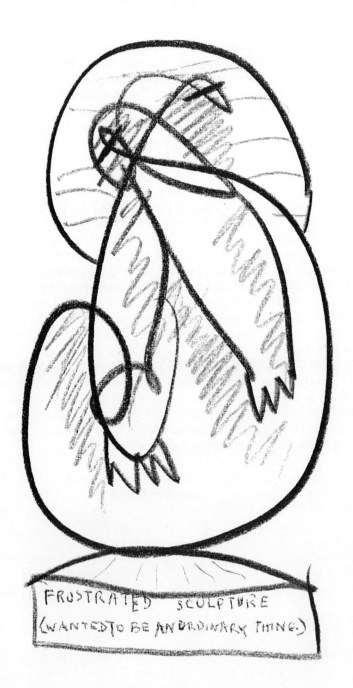

FRUSTRATED SCULPTURE
(WANTED TO BE AN ORDINARY THING.)

# Donald Woods Winnicott 1896–1971

The British psychoanalyst, Donald Woods Winnicott, brought a new dimension to psychoanalysis by virtue of his paediatric training, his ability to communicate with the archaic levels of the personality, and the originality of his mind. His long experience of the psychoanalysis and psychotherapy of both children and adults whose psychical structures were not those of the classical neuroses enabled him to develop concepts of his own and to introduce useful technical innovations for cases that do not respond to the usual psychoanalytical approach.

After being ignored in France for many years, the works of D. W. Winnicott are now reaching an ever-wider audience. The sometimes passionate interest aroused by these works is no doubt due to the new light they shed on the human psyche and to the therapeutic possibilities they offer paediatricians, psychoanalysts, social workers, educationalists, teachers, and parents.

All those who have studied or commented on Winnicott's work, either in order to develop their clinical work, or to enrich psychoanalytical theory, have stressed, above all, his originality and nonconformism. There can be no doubt that in reading Winnicott's works one is struck at once by the originality of a thought that, while remaining faithful, in broad outline, to the theories of Freud, and to a certain extent, to those of Melanie

Klein, never remains within a rigid, orthodox approach, when clinical facts or the observation of children and parents have required a broadening of existing theories.

Through his background, Winnicott was probably destined to play this role of rebel, caring little for theoretical models, to which he referred, of course, but only in so far as what he discovered in his contact with children allowed him to accept them – otherwise he was quite prepared to ignore them. It is precisely for this reason that he is praised by some and blamed by others. By background, we mean, of course, his professional training and his first experience of adult life, but also his family background.

D. W. Winnicott was born in 1896 into a comfortably off Plymouth family. In the huge house surrounded by a large garden, the young Donald, the only boy in the family, was not alone: he had two elder sisters. In the house next door lived four cousins – two boys and two girls – with whom he played and went for walks. His parents, who provided both affection and security, were great art lovers and all the members of the family loved music. One of Winnicott's sisters became a painter. Donald also had a 'nanny', for whom he felt great affection and gratitude throughout his life. This 'last-born' might have become a horrible 'spoilt child', tyrannical and unhappy. He was nothing of the kind. Indeed, his parents' great love did not exclude the exercise of authority. His father knew how to show calm firmness when necessary. Thus, the day when Donald, aged twelve, swore on returning from school, his father decided to send him away to boarding school for the next academic year. As an adult, Winnicott was grateful to his father for that display of authority, which enabled him to assume his ambivalence towards the father figure. However, he believed that his father, who devoted a lot of his time to his own business and to the affairs of the city of which he was twice mayor, had not made his presence sufficiently felt during his early childhood. One day, he confided to his wife Clare Winnicott: 'So my father was there to kill and be killed, but it is probably true that in my early years he left me too much to all my mothers. Things never quite righted themselves.'[1]

At sixteen, after a fractured collar-bone, D. W. Winnicott

decided to become a doctor, so that, he thought at the time, he would never have to depend on a doctor if ill or injured, though he suspected that this would disappoint his father, who wanted him to follow in his footsteps in the family business. At Cambridge, he studied biology and medicine. Then came World War I. He was mobilized as an assistant nurse at Cambridge and was thus able to continue his studies, but he was unhappy to see his friends sent off to the front while he stayed on in a hospital. As soon as he could, he joined the navy and was made a student surgeon on a destroyer.

After the war, Winnicott went back to the university. He had always wanted to go into general practice in the country, but one day, in a bookshop, he discovered a book by Freud, leafed through it, bought it, read it, and felt that psychoanalysis was what he was looking for. He had always taken an interest in children and was appointed consultant in general medicine (paediatrics did not then exist as a special branch of medicine). He decided to undergo analysis. In 1923, D. W. Winnicott took on two consultancies, one at the Queen's Hospital for Children, the other at the Paddington Green Children's Hospital, where he practised for forty years. His two paediatric consultations soon became paedo-psychiatric consultations, in which Winnicott dealt with family conflicts, helping parents and children to communicate better with one another, enabling them to resolve the unconscious conflicts that prevented good relationships and the child's development.

One has to have seen Winnicott at work to understand how he was able to be so receptive to the unconscious, to the archaic levels of the personality. Acute intuition enabled him to find immediately, during psychotherapeutic interviews or during analysis, the sometimes apparently paradoxical sentence that would allow the patient, adult, or child, to find himself in communication with the most secret parts of himself. The first time I attended his consultation at Paddington Green Children's Hospital, I (Anne Clancier) was amazed at the ease with which Winnicott got into contact with the child. On that particular day, indeed, one of the children brought to the consultation refused any contact. He stood in the corner of the room, motionless, silent, refusing to look anybody in the eye. Winnicott sat on the

3

floor a certain distance from the child, picked up a bundle of small squares of paper and a pencil, while another pencil was placed on the floor near the pile of papers. Very quickly, Winnicott drew what he called a 'squiggle', talking as he did so; the child got interested in what he was doing and came closer. Winnicott, as if he were continuing a conversation that had already begun, asked the little boy to complete the drawing. After a while, the child drew a line on the same paper; Winnicott then continued the drawing, commenting as he did so, then he took another piece of paper and asked the child to start the game (for it is always through games technique that Winnicott communicates with such children). The boy also drew a squiggle, which Winnicott then completed, then it was his turn to start a new squiggle on a new piece of paper (at first they were not figurative designs), which the little boy completed, and so on, each beginning or finishing the drawing in turn. Winnicott said a few words after each drawing. The squiggles thus became meaningful and, through his comments, Winnicott gave the child an interpretation, in the psychoanalytical sense of the term. By moving from gesture and drawing to language, he enabled the child to begin to elaborate his unconscious fantasies through the medium of the squiggle. I realized that each of the drawings begun by Winnicott could suggest a symbolic object: a snake, a bird, an egg, an arrow, a boat, etc.

Depending on the way in which the child completed the drawing, Winnicott grasped the level of the preconscious fantasy and was able to give the interpretation that seemed useful to him at that moment. After the consultation, Winnicott was willing to answer the questions of those who had come to study with him; in a few sentences he made clear what had seemed to him to be significant in the particular case and what he had been aiming at by his intervention. I was struck by Winnicott's ease of manner, naturalness, and simplicity. He had about him none of the conformism of many leading figures in the medical world; he never seemed to be speaking from a professorial chair. Yet one left enriched, filled with admiration and respect, as if one had had the privilege of being in the presence of a grandfather who combined wisdom with kindness. All those who have worked with Winnicott say much the same thing. Only narcissistic or rigid personalities, who appreciate social conventions and formal frameworks more than intuition, fantasy, and humour, could have been incapable of perceiving Winnicott's personal genius. Dr Sacha Nacht was very fond of him. One day, after returning from London, I told him of my admiration for Winnicott. 'He's crazy, but he's a genius!' he exclaimed. Winnicott himself thought that to be crazy in this sense – the light, everyday sense, of course – enabled one to communicate with the deepest parts of the psyche. To reject the possibility of regressing was to impoverish oneself, to cut oneself off from the vital sources that emanate from the unconscious and are at the source of all creativity. One day he came out with a sentence that sounded truly Shakespearean: 'We are poor indeed if we are only sane.'

2nd November 1964.

# 1 There's no such thing as an infant!

In expounding Winnicott's ideas, we shall follow the way that he himself proposed when he tried to explain his method, or rather his way of developing his ideas. In the revised edition of his *Collected Papers*, published under the title *Through Paediatrics to Psychoanalysis*, he says:

> 'I shall not give an historical survey and show the development of my ideas from the theories of others, because my mind does not work that way. What happens is that I gather this and that, here and there, settle down to clinical experience, form my own theories and then, last of all, interest myself in looking to see where I stole what. Perhaps this is as good a method as any.'[1]

So let us follow Winnicott, gathering in his works those points that strike us as essential; we shall then try to see how, out of clinical facts and the concepts that he gradually developed, he built up his theory. It was no accident that Winnicott makes this remark at the beginning of his essay 'Primitive Emotional Development', which we shall now examine.

Winnicott, who concerned himself early on with the phase preceding the first object relationship, once burst out at a meeting of the Psychoanalytical Society: 'There is no such thing as an infant!' Concerned at hearing himself come out with such a statement, he tried to give his reasons: he explained that, when he was shown a baby, he was also shown someone who took care of that baby, or at least a pram to which the eyes and ears of someone were glued. One was in the presence of a 'nursing couple'.[2] Starting with this intuition, Winnicott tried to understand what clinical observations lay behind what he had said. It seemed to him that what preceded object relationships was presented in the following way: 'The unit is not the individual, the unit is an environment–individual set-up. The centre of gravity of the being does not start off in the individual. It is in the total set-up.'[3]

It is certain that this discovery is bound up with Winnicott's paediatric experience. Other psychoanalysts, most of whom at the time were concerned with adult neurotics, had paid very little attention to the child's first relations with its mother, whereas Winnicott places them at the centre of his work. In the children's hospital in which he practised as a paediatrician, he set up and ran a psychoanalytical consultation.

How, then, on the basis of the nursing couple, is the child to be able to develop? Winnicott explains: 'With a good-enough technique, the centre of gravity of being in the environment–individual set-up can afford to lodge in the centre, in the kernel rather than in the shell. The human being now developing an entity from the centre can be localized in the baby's body.'[4] In short, the 'nursing couple' constitutes for Winnicott a dyad. When things go well, this dyad evolves without setbacks, and the child develops quite naturally. When things go badly, there are distortions in the relationship between the two elements of the dyad and psychical disturbances, neurotic or psychotic, may later appear.

Two factors are of particular importance in this dyad: on the one hand the personal factor of the child, the terrain, and the process of maturation, and, on the other, the facilitating environment. Here Winnicott is close to Freud.

In 'Formulations on the Two Principles of Mental Functioning' (1911), Freud writes:

> 'It will rightly be objected that an organization which was a slave to the pleasure-principle and neglected the reality of the external world could not maintain itself alive for the shortest

time, so that it could not have come into existence at all. The employment of a fiction like this is, however, justified when one considers that the infant – provided one includes with it the care it receives from its mother – does almost realize a psychical system of this kind. It probably hallucinates the fulfilment of its internal needs; it betrays its unpleasure, when there is an increase of stimulus and an absence of satisfaction, by the motor discharge of screaming and beating about with its arms and legs, and it then experiences the satisfaction it has hallucinated. Later, as an older child, it learns to employ these manifestations of discharge intentionally as methods of expressing its feelings. Since the later care of children is modelled on the care of infants, the dominance of the pleasure-principle can really come to an end only when a child has achieved complete psychical detachment from its parents.'[5]

Commenting on this text by Freud, Winnicott adds: 'The words: "provided one includes with it the care it receives from its mother" have great importance in the context of this study. The infant and the maternal care together form a unit.'

## Parental care

Satisfactory parental care may be classified roughly into three overlapping stages:

1. Holding.
2. Mother and infant living together. Here the father's function (of dealing with the environment of the mother) is not known to the infant.
3. Father, mother, and infant, all three living together.

Winnicott stresses that there is an innate potential in each baby, but that the baby can become a child only if it is coupled with maternal care.

HOLDING AND THE NORMALLY DEVOTED MOTHER

According to Winnicott, the term 'holding' denotes not only the actual physical holding of the infant, but also the total environmental provision prior to the concept of *living with* – in other words, before the notion of two and three is introduced. This notion 'includes the management of experiences that are inherent in existence' and which occur in the period in which the psychological field is 'determined by the awareness and empathy of the mother'.[6] Later will occur what Winnicott calls 'living together', which implies object relationships and the emergence of the child from the state of fusion with the mother, and therefore the beginnings, one might say, of the formation of the ego.

Winnicott gave examples of this, when, in his broadcasts, he tried to get mothers and fathers to appreciate the needs of their children.

> 'Enjoy yourself!' he exclaimed, addressing the mother. 'Enjoy finding out new things about yourself. Enjoy having more right than you have ever had before to do just what you feel is good. Enjoy being annoyed with the baby when cries and yells prevent acceptance of the milk that you long to be generous with. Enjoy all sorts of womanly feelings that you cannot even start to explain to a man. Particularly, I know you will enjoy the signs that gradually appear that the baby is a person, and that you are recognized as a person by the baby. Enjoy all this for your own sake, but the pleasure which you can get out of the messy business of infant care happens to be vitally important from the baby's point of view. The baby does not want to be given the correct feed at the correct time so much as to be fed by someone who loves feeding her own baby. The baby takes for granted all things like the softness of the clothes and having the bathwater at the right temperature. What cannot be taken for granted is the mother's pleasure that goes with the clothing and bathing of her own baby. If you are there enjoying it all, it is like the sun coming out, for the baby. The mother's pleasure has to be there or else the whole procedure is dead, useless, and mechanical.'[7]

In the simplest possible terms, Winnicott encourages mothers not to feel guilty by showing them that the pleasure that they experience with their baby is crucially important:

'The real trouble is that so great feelings of pleasure belong to the intimate, bodily, and spiritual bond that can exist between a mother and her baby that mothers easily fall a prey to the advice of people who seem to say that such feelings must not be indulged in. Surely the modern puritan is to be found in this realm of infant feeding! Fancy keeping a baby away from his mother after he is born till he has lost his one possibility (through his sense of smell) of feeling he has found her again, after he had lost her! Fancy wrapping up the baby while he is feeding so that he cannot handle the breasts, or the bottle, with the result that he can only take part in the proceedings by 'Yes' (sucking) or 'No' (turning the head away or sleeping)! Fancy starting out feeding a baby by the clock before he has gained a feeling that there really is anything outside himself and his desires at all.'[8]

## Infant development during the holding phase

Winnicott posits a notion, that of the 'good-enough mother', which he is very fond of and which excludes any sentimentality. For a mother to be good enough, the environment must be good enough, that is to say, the father must be supportive of the mother; during this stage, development will proceed normally and various Freudian notions, such as the primary process, primary identification, and auto-eroticism will become 'living realities'.

Associated with the attainment of 'unit status', providing development is normal, the infant will gradually conquer and preserve 'the capacity for re-experiencing unintegrated states, but this depends on the continuation of reliable maternal care or on the build-up in the infant of memories of maternal care beginning gradually to be perceived as such.'[9] It seems that Winnicott is referring here to the gradual constitution of an ego. For him, the psyche and the soma are closely linked: the infant's psychosomatic existence takes shape and begins to take on a personal pattern; this is what is called the psyche indwelling in the soma.

One might note here the importance of the relationship between the skin and the ego.

'As a further development there comes into existence what might be called a limiting membrane, which to some extent (in health) is equated with the surface of the skin, and has a position between the infant's 'me' and his 'not-me'. So the infant comes to have an inside and an outside, and a body-scheme. In this way meaning comes to the function of intake and output; moreover, it gradually becomes meaningful to postulate a personal or inner psychic reality for the infant.'[10]

Thus one can glimpse in these lines Winnicott's conception of the containing function of the mother and of the skin. Even for the 'well-held' infant when very young, the skin cannot serve as a container if the mother does not herself contain it physically and psychically. This is one of the roles of the mother that child analysts are stressing more and more today.

According to Winnicott, the child will pass in a few months from a state of absolute dependence, in which he does not even have the means of recognizing maternal care, to a state of relative dependence in which he begins to take account of his need of maternal care and to differentiate himself from his mother; lastly he will develop by moving towards a state of independence that will never be satisfactory if the child has not at the outset been able to have confidence in a dependable environment. We shall see later how the self is established.

HANDLING

Handling is the way of caring for a child, that is to say, a relationship that is both more limited and closer than holding, which is bound up with the environment in the wider sense. The way of caring for the infant, feeding him, washing him, etc., is also very important, but it may be said of this handling what has already been said: that it is essentially bound up with the mother–infant relationship and with the relationship between a father and this relationship, it may also be said that today fathers concern themselves a great deal more with infants and the way they care for them is important. They help to protect the mother and the baby against whatever tends to intrude into their bond, the bond that constitutes the essence and very nature of maternal care.

THE PRESENTATION OF THE OBJECT

The world is presented to the infant by the mother. The infant cannot at first distinguish itself from the mother, he cannot distinguish the outside world from the inside world, nor can he at first distinguish between the real world and the imaginary world. The mother must gradually help him to make these distinctions; she must not present him too suddenly with fragments of the world that are too large. Winnicott explained this in a concrete way when he addressed mothers directly:

'The mother is sharing a specialized bit of the world with her small child, keeping that bit small enough so that the child is not muddled, yet enlarging it very gradually so that the growing capacity of the child to enjoy the world is catered for. . . . There are two things that a mother does which help here. One is that she takes the trouble to avoid coincidences.'[11]

Coincidences lead to muddle. Examples would be handing a baby over to someone else's care at the same time as weaning, or introducing solids during an attack of measles, and so on. 'The other thing is that she is able to distinguish between fact and fantasy.'[12]

Thus when the child has a nightmare and calls out to his mother, even though he is beginning to wake up, he may, for instance, think that she is a witch. In other words, the child's fantasy world is very susceptible to the way in which the mother has helped him to become aware of the external world and of the imaginary world, and of the way in which she herself has integrated these two domains:

'So a great deal depends on the way the world is presented to the infant and to the growing child. The ordinary mother can start and carry through this amazing business of introducing the world in small doses, not because she is clever, like the philosophers, but simply because of the devotion she feels for her own baby.'[13]

Thus the mother assists in the establishment of the faculties of symbolization in the child. On this suject, Winnicott refers to the work of Mme Sechehaye, who says that when she gave her patient an apple at the right moment (symbolic realization), it did not matter whether the patient ate the apple, or just looked at it, or took it and kept it. 'The important thing was that the patient was able to create an object, and Sechehaye did no more than enable the object to take apple-shape, so that the girl had created a part of the actual world, an apple.'[14]

## Becoming a person

### DEVELOPMENT OF THE INDIVIDUAL IN A FACILITATING ENVIRONMENT

Winnicott shows that the psychical unity of the development of the infant is established in various ways. He takes as his starting point Glover's work on the ego nuclei and the formation of the ego.[15] Depending on whether these nuclei achieve integration or remain in a state of sub-integration, the ego is constituted in a satisfactory or unsatisfactory way. In order to grasp the unstable equilibrium in which the ego exists at the beginning of its formation, Winnicott takes as an example the character of Lewis Carroll's Humpty Dumpty. 'He has just achieved integration into one whole thing, and has emerged from the environment–individual set-up so that he is perched on a wall, no longer devotedly held.'[16]

Winnicott then refers to the works of Melanie Klein concerning the schizo-paranoid position in emotional development. He believes that his own clinical observations corroborate her descriptions. At the beginning of his life the child undergoes terrible anxieties, in a paranoid state, against which he defends himself as best he can. Some psychotic children do not manage to emerge from this stage. Winnicott analyses the counter-transference of these children's therapist. One feels subjected to omnipotent control, but not control from a strong central point. 'It is a world of magic, and one feels mad to be in it.' Those who treat psychotic children of this kind 'know how mad we have to be to inhabit this world' and one can practise psychotherapy only if one agrees to share this world for a long period. This view is also close to that of Marion Milner.[17]

*'Aggression in Relation to Emotional Development'*[18]

For Winnicott, aggression pre-exists the integration of the

personality. He links primary aggression with motility and refers to the work of the French analysts P. Marty and M. Fain.[19] Winnicott provides several examples; the baby who kicks in his mother's belly or who chews her breast with his gums is not trying, it seems, to destroy or to hurt. 'At origin aggressiveness is almost synonymous with activity; it is a matter of part-function.' When the child becomes a person, he gradually organizes his part functions into aggression. 'Oral eroticism gathers to itself aggressive components and in health it is oral love that carries the basis of the greater part of actual aggressiveness – that is, aggression intended by the individual and felt as such by the people around.'

For Winnicott all experience is both physical and non-physical. Ideas accompany and enrich bodily function, while 'bodily functioning accompanies and realizes ideation'.

Winnicott describes three stages of aggression in terms of stages in ego development:

(1) an early stage of pre-integration, in which purpose is sought without concern;
(2) an intermediate stage in which there is integration and in which purpose is sought with concern; guilt now appears;
(3) lastly, the stage of the total personality.

Interpersonal relationships, and the triangular situation in particular, are established with the appearance of conscious and unconscious conflicts.

The individual arrives at what Winnicott calls the 'stage of concern', which he relates to Melanie Klein's 'depressive position'. With this position appears the capacity to feel guilty; thus part of aggressiveness gives birth to the social functions.

*Frustration*

Frustration is inevitable in all experience; it may encourage the dichotomy between innocent aggressive impulses towards frustrating objects and guilt-productive aggressive impulses towards good objects. From Winnicott's work it emerges that frustration must be minimal, in proportion to the child's capacity to assume it.

In the management of the child's inner world, the role of the parents is crucial, not only that of the mother at the outset, but that of both parents. If the mother is not supported by her husband or if the parents quarrel, disorders of the personality will follow. Winnicott cites in particular the case of parents who quarrel in front of the child at an age when he finds it difficult to master this experience; he then introjects the image of the parents quarrelling and uses up a great deal of energy mastering this bad internalized relationship. Clinically, the child may feel tired, depressed, or even be physically ill. Sometimes, at certain moments, the child will behave 'as if possessed' by the quarrelling parents and may well become, in a compulsive way, aggressive, unreasonable, and even sometimes hallucinate. This behaviour is related to the mechanism described by Anna Freud as identification with the aggressor.[20]

Although frustration must be minimal, it is more or less indispensable, for, in order to develop, the child needs to find opposition. 'Crudely, it needs something to push against, unless it is to remain unexperienced and a threat to well-being. In health, however, by definition, the individual can enjoy going around looking for appropriate opposition.'[21]

### 'THE DEPRESSIVE POSITION IN NORMAL EMOTIONAL DEVELOPMENT'

In this article of 1954–55, Winnicott situates his ideas in relationship to the theory of Melanie Klein.

Let us remember what Melanie Klein meant by *position*: 'Certain configurations of object-relations and libido-distribution through which the individual passes during development.' Melanie Klein describes two positions, the paranoid and the depressive. A distinction is drawn between them and the stages of libidinal development, for they refer to the relations between fantasy and object-relationship rather than to 'attachment of one particular object and erotogenic zone'.[23] These positions are situated in the first year of life, the depressive position following the paranoid-schizoid position roughly between six and eight months. The depressive position arrives when the infant 'realizes that both his love and hate are directed

16

towards the same object – the mother – becomes aware of his ambivalence and concern to protect her from his hate and to make reparations for what damage he imagines his hate has done.'[24]

In this article, Winnicott describes his own description of the depressive position, a concept that he takes up from Melanie Klein. He goes on to say that he has studied the Kleinian points of view, for he found them useful in his work with children, and he reminds us that he received instruction from her from 1935 and 1940 in case supervision.

Winnicott describes the depressive position as the culmination of the process of the child's emotional development. When the child has been through the depressive position, he is capable of interpersonal relationships, and of course he will remain capable of them when he becomes an adult. On the other hand, the child (or adult) who has not achieved the depressive position in his personal development will never achieve satisfactory integration of his personality and the establishment of a relationship with the environment. We have pointed out how the infant needs to be 'held' by a mother who adapts herself to the ego's needs. When he arrives at the depressive position, he still needs to be held by the mother. Winnicott expresses the importance of the time factor, for the mother must hold the situation for several months so that the infant 'has the chance to work through the consequences of instinctual experiences'.

The depressive position is a critical period in the life of any infant. The mother who has constantly held the situation 'enables the infant's coexisting love and hate to become sorted out and interrelated and gradually brought under control from within in a way that is healthy'.[25]

Winnicott believes that this depressive position coincides with weaning or the beginning of weaning. By way of example, he says[26] that suckling may sometimes seem to the infant to be a terrible time, for 'instinctual demands can be fierce and frightening. . . . Being hungry is like being possessed by wolves'. When the infant has reached nine months, he is used to these demands and is now capable of controlling himself even while these instinctual urges hold sway. 'The baby has even become able to acknowledge the urges as a part of what it means to be a person alive.' The mother is then perceived as a person, 'as something attractive and valued exactly as she appears. How awful to be hungry and to feel oneself ruthlessly attacking this same mother.' So, very often, babies lose their appetite at this point.

At this same period, about seven, eight, or nine months, the baby begins to play and to drop objects. According to Winnicott this is a very important game and one that often exasperates mothers. Yet the aim really is to use the baby's developing ability to get rid of things. As we shall see later, it is important, therefore, to choose the moment for weaning.

So that the depressive position can be reached and passed the mother must be able to be regarded as a total person and the child be able to feel himself to be a total person.

Winnicott then proposed to regard the depressed position as the *stage of concern*, considering that the infant is ruthless, that is to say, has no concern as to the consequences of his instinctual needs, for love and instinct seem to be identical at this time. There then follows a stage that he calls *pre-ruth* that is to say, prior to compassion and concern, and lastly, the stage of ruth or concern.

### The function of environment

Gradually the child differentiates between two images of the mother, one highly agreeable, so valued in the quiet phases, and the other who will be ruthlessly attacked in the phases of need and excitement.

'Two things are happening. One is the perception of the identity of the two objects, the mother of the quiet phases and the mother used and even attacked at the instinctual climax. The other is the beginning of the recognition of the existence of ideas, fantasy, imaginative elaboration of the function, the acceptance of ideas and of fantasy related to fact but not to be confused with fact.

'Such complex progression in emotional development of the individual cannot be made without good-enough environmental health. The latter is here represented by the survival of the mother. Until the child has collected memory material there is no room for the mother's disappearance.'[27]

The baby 'puts one and one together and begins to see that the answer is one, and not two. The mother of the dependent relationship (anaclitic) is also the object of instinctual (biologically driven) love. For the baby is 'fobbed off by the feed itself; instinct tension disappears, and the baby is both satisfied and cheated'.

*Depressive anxiety*

'Instinctual experience brings the baby two types of anxiety. The first is this that I have described: anxiety about the object of instinctual love. The mother is not the same after as before.' Winnicott tries to imagine what the babies feel: 'There is a hole, where previously there was a full body of richness.'

'The other anxiety is of the infant's own inside. The infant has had an experience and does not feel the same as before.' Gradually the baby has fantasies concerning what is happening inside him. He has 'already become a person with a limiting membrane, an inside and an outside'. It is in this way that the self is gradually formed. The child then becomes capable of sorting out things, that is to say, he is able to separate good from bad, inside from outside.

Winnicott sums up the various psychical operations that now take place thus:

1. A relation between infant and mother complicated by instinctual experience.
2. A dim perception of the effect (hole).
3. An inner working-through, the results of experience being sorted out.
4. A capacity to give, because of the sorting out of the good and bad within.
5. Reparation.

A benign circle is then formed. 'The infant becomes able to tolerate the hole' (a consequence of instinctual love). There now occurs the beginning of *guilt* feeling.[28] Winnicott explains that guilt starts through the bringing together of the two mothers, the mother of love and the mother of hate, and that this feeling gradually grows to be a healthy and normal source of activity in relationships. This is 'one source of potency, and of social contribution, and of artistic performance (but not of art itself, which has roots at a deeper level).' We shall see later what Winnicott regards as the other sources of art.

Winnicott shows that these developmental phases are re-experienced in adult analysis, for example

> 'when the depressive position is reached in the transference. We see an expression of love followed by anxiety about the analyst and also by hypochondriacal fears. Or we see, more positively, a release of instinct, and a development towards richness in the personality, and an increase in potency or in general potential for social contribution.'

> 'The depressions that are encountered clinically in psychiatry are chiefly not of the type that is related to the "depressive position".'

What we see appearing here is the concept of the false self, which we shall study later.

> 'If in an individual the depressive position has been achieved and fully established, then the reaction to loss is *grief* or *sadness*. Where there is some degree of failure of the depressive position, the result of loss is depression.'

### THE MANIC DEFENCE

In classical psychoanalysis, the manic defence, as described by Melanie Klein,[29] is a form of defensive behaviour exhibited by persons who defend themselves against anxiety, guilt, and depression by

(a) denial of the guilt, anxiety, and depression;
(b) the operation of a fantasy of omnipotent control, by means of which they imagine themselves to be in control of all situations which might provoke anxiety or feelings of help-lessness;

(c)  identification with objects from whom a sense of power can be borrowed; and

(d)  projection of 'bad' aspects of the self on to others.[30]

It should be noted that, years before writing his article on the depressive position, Winnicott had studied the manic defence, for the first work that he published as a psychoanalyst, in 1935, had as its title 'The Manic Defence'.[31]

It may be said that the manic defence is a denial of inner reality and that it is a part of one's own manic defence 'to be unable to give full significance to inner reality'. Winnicott points out that the depressed subject is aware of being depressed, whereas the subject with manic defences has no awareness of his defensive attitude, since he is fleeing from inner reality and therefore observation of himself. Winnicott shows the various characteristics of the manic defence:

(a)  Flight to external reality from inner reality.

(b)  Denial of inner reality.

(c)  Holding the people of the inner reality in 'suspended animation'.

(d)  Denial of the sensations of depression.

He shows that, during psychotherapy or psychoanalysis, depression may be confronted and elaborated if the manic defences are allowed to diminish.

Winnicott provides several clinical cases.

As an example of the manic defence when the patient feels dead inside and sees the world as a colourless place, we shall cite the case of David.

David showed the flight from inner reality to the interest in the surface of his body and in his surface feelings. Thus he had been called an asocial child with 'sex and lavatory obsession'. Aged eight, the only child of a depressive father and of a mother who, though highly neurotic, was also very anxious about the situation at home and gave the therapist very good support, David was liked for a short period by everyone with whom he did not come into contact with very much. At one of the earliest sessions, he said: 'I hope that I am not tiring you.' This prepared Winnicott for an exhausting case. He soon became aware that David was trying to tire him. After a few sessions, David fled from the anxieties belonging to deep fantasies that his games with small toys had revealed. He began to show an interest in the world outside the window and beyond the therapist's door – especially the lift. The inside of the room had become his own inside and if he were to deal with the therapist and the contents of his room (father and mother, witches, ghosts, persecutors, etc.) he would have to have the means to control them. First he had to tire them out, as he feared he could not control them – and Winnicott felt that this showed some distrust in his omnipotence. Alongside the need to tire the therapist out, there developed a desire to save him from exhaustion, so as a slave-driver he took immense care that his slave should not become exhausted.

Soon it became clear that it was he who was becoming exhausted and the problem of the analyst becoming tired was gradually solved by the interpretations in regard to his own exhaustion in the control of the internalized parents, who were exhausting each other as well as him. Winnicott says,

'I was fortunate enough to have him in my room at 11 a.m. on Armistice Day. The matter of Armistice Day observance interested him vastly; it was not so much that his father had fought in the war as that he had already developed (before analysis and in relation to the analysis) an interest in the streets and the traffic, as providing a not hopelessly uncontrollable sample of inner reality.

'He came full of the pleasure of buying a poppy from a lady and at 11 o'clock he was interested in every detail of the street events. Then came the long-awaited two-minutes' silence. It was a particularly complete silence in my neighbourhood and he was absolutely delighted. "Isn't it lovely!" For two minutes in his life he felt as if he was not tired, as he need not tire out the parents, since there had come along an omnipotent control imposed from outside and accepted as real by all.

'Of interest was his fantasy that during the silence the ladies went on selling flowers, the only permitted activity; a more manic, internal omnipotence would have stopped everything (the good included).'

Subsequently, analysis of the depressive position and of the manic defence were followed by moments of intense tiredness, sadness, and hopelessness, in which he showed indirect evidence of guilt feelings. He became very frightened. There was a moment when he illustrated his resistance by getting the therapist to teach him diving, which in fact he refused to learn. Winnicott had to say to him: 'Here you are wasting my time! How can I teach you to dive if you can't stand? I am very angry with you' – and so on and so on. All this became a tremendous joke and he made his therapist laugh heartily and was then very pleased. But he was aware that this joking was part of the defence against the depressive position and guilt feelings. How could he dive into the inside of the body, and therefore meet his mother's depression by diving into her inner world, if he could not stand up, be sure that he was alive, understand what he would find inside?

'David's case illustrates the ego's danger from the bad inner objects, the boy fearing lest he will be emptied and exhausted by the inner parents who constantly emptied each other; hence his interest in the bodies and feelings of other children. The progress of his analysis also illustrates the importance of an understanding of the mechanism of the omnipotent control of the internal objects, and of the relation of denial of tiredness, anxiety, and guilt feelings to denial of inner reality.'

THE CAPACITY TO BE ALONE

In the psychoanalytical literature more has been written on the *fear* of being alone or the *wish* to be alone than on the *ability* to be alone. Distinguishing this attitude from the withdrawn state,[32] a defensive organization implying an expectation of persecution, Winnicott discusses the positive aspects of the capacity to be alone, which is one of the important signs of mature emotional development, in his article: 'The Capacity to be Alone' (1958).[33] He makes reference to Freud's concept concerning the *anaclitic relationship* (1914) and bases his arguments on the observation, during psychoanalytical treatment, of a silent phase or a silent session, and this silence, 'far from being evidence of resistance, turns out to be an achievement on the part of the patient'.

Closely linked with emotional maturity, the very foundation of the capacity to be alone is *paradoxical*, since it is a capacity to be alone in the presence of someone.

The capacity to be alone is based on various experiences. Thus the child may be separated from his mother only when he has 'had enough', but one experience is crucial, and 'this experience is that of being alone, as an infant and small child, in the presence of mother'.

To describe this type of relationship between the infant or small child and the mother or her substitute, persons who may be trusted, Winnicott invents a term, *ego-relatedness*, which he contrasts with *id-relationship* which is 'a recurring complication in what might be called ego life'. 'Ego-relatedness,' he says, 'refers to the relationship between two people, one of whom at any rate is alone; perhaps both are alone, yet the presence of each is important to the other.' He illustrates his argument by comparing the words *like* and *love*: 'Liking is a matter of ego-relatedness, whereas loving is more a matter of id-relationships, either crude or in sublimated form.' Winnicott reminds us that lack of id-tension may produce anxiety, but that time-integration of the personality enables the individual to wait for the natural return of id-tension, and to enjoy sharing solitude, that is to say, solitude that is relatively free from the property that we call 'withdrawal', after sexual intercourse, for example.

To illustrate this let us cite an incident recounted by a patient: one day, when she was feeling particularly loving and close to her husband she said to him: 'What I find marvellous about you is that when I'm with you I feel alone.' What she meant was that she felt herself, natural, without having to put on a mask, as she often did in her social relationships. But her husband did not understand, felt wounded and aggressive towards her. Probably only one of the two partners had acquired the capacity to be alone in the presence of others; furthermore that person expressed her feeling that her self could be revealed in that relationship, whereas a false self held the stage in her other relationships. This example may also illustrate Winnicott's theories on the self, which we shall approach later.

Winnicott also thinks that 'an individual's capacity to be alone depends on his ability to deal with the feelings aroused by the primal scene'. The healthy child who sees or imagines sexual excitement between his parents will be able to master the hate and canalize it into masturbation, where responsibility, for the fantasy, may be accepted by the child, who is the third person in a triangular relationship. To be able to be alone in these circumstances implies a maturity of erotic development, a fusion of the aggressive and erotic impulses, and it implies a tolerance of ambivalence and a capacity to identify with each of the parents. Winnicott sees this capacity to be alone, therefore, as a sign of emotional maturity.

Innumerable clinical cases involving both children and adults, whose major symptom is boredom, confirm Winnicott's views. In analysing these cases, one always finds anxiety when confronting the aggressive fantasies associated with the primal scene.[34]

One can also see in such cases the moroseness of adolescence studied by Pierre Mâle.[35]

*Ego-relatedness* is very important for Winnicott, for it is 'the stuff out of which friendship is made. It may turn out to be the *matrix of transference*.' He believes that an 'id-impulse is signifi- cant only if it is contained in ego living'; it 'either disrupts a weak ego or else strengthens a strong one. It is possible to say that id-relationships strengthen the ego when they occur in a framework of ego-relatedness.'

When the infant is alone (in the presence of someone), he is able to do the equivalent of what in an adult world would be called relaxing, he is

'able to become unintegrated, to flounder, to be in a state in which there is no orientation, to be able to exist for a time without being either a reactor to an external impingement or an active person with a direction of interest or movement. The stage is set for an id experience. In the course of time there arrives a sensation or an impulse. In this setting the sensation or impulse will feel real and be truly a personal experience.'

It is important that 'there is someone available, someone pres- ent, although present without making demands'. Later, the individual will be able to forego the *actual* presence of a mother or mother-figure. This marks the stage of the establishment of an 'internal environment'.

This article is crucial in the understanding of Winnicott's concepts of the transitional area, the area of play, the construc- tion of the self and of the false self.

Lastly, Winnicott posits the hypothesis of an *ego orgasm*, a concept that he bases on certain experiences of adult life: for example, the satisfaction experienced at a concern, or in the theatre, or in friendship, a satisfaction that he tries to distinguish from the concept of sublimation. Here his demon- stration is less convincing, though it is true that sublimation is still, even today, one of the most controversial concepts in psychoanalysis.

# 2 The child and his fantasies

## The establishment of a self

'At first the individual is not the unit. As perceived from outside the unit is an environment–individual set-up. The outsider knows that the individual's psyche can only start in a certain setting. In this setting the individual can gradually come to create a personal environment.'[1] (Winnicott adds in a footnote, 'according to my view the concept of the body-scheme as put forward by Scott (1949) concerns only the individual, and not the unit named here the environment-individual set-up.') It is through the environment that the child will be able to pass gradually from a state of absolute dependence first to a state of relative dependence, then to a state of independence.

In 'Psychoses and Child Care', Winnicott makes a comparison between the maternal attitude in the primitive stages of emotional development and that of analysis with very regressed patients.

Close study of the earliest development of the 'psyche-soma', which occurs during the stage of building up the 'environment-individual' set-up and while emerging from that stage, is illustrated by two diagrams (*Figures 1* and *2*).

The emergence of id impulses makes it easier for the child to face the outside world. If the good breast realizes this experience

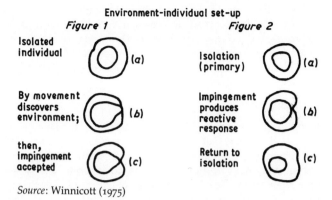

Source: Winnicott (1975)

of itself, all will go well. When the two do not meet, there will be a split.

On this subject it might be worth remembering E. Bick's paper, 'The Experience of the Skin in Early Object-relations',[2] given at the 25th International Congress of Psychoanalysis (Copenhagen, 1967). According to E. Bick, the skin has a primary function: to maintain the parts of the personality that, in their more primitive form, are unable to be connected to one another. This function of the skin as limit, as containing the parts of the self, rests on the introjection of an external object, experienced as capable of assuming it. Later, identification with this object-function makes possible the fantasy of internal and external spaces.

The concept of space, of space inside the self, cannot come about unless the containing functions have been introjected.

The stage of split and of the primitive idealizations of the self and of the object depend, therefore, on this earlier process by which the self and the object are contained by their respective 'skins'. E. Bick cites cases in which the need for a containing object seems to produce in the unintegrated infantile state a quest for an object that may be felt, temporarily at least, as holding together the parts of the personality. According to the clinical material, this containing object is experienced concretely as a skin. Disturbances in the function of the primitive skin may lead to the development of a 'second skin': dependence on the object is then replaced by a pseudo-independence, by the inadequate use of certain mental functions and even in innate talents, with a view to creating a substitute for this containing function of the skin.

Mention might also be made here of D. Anzieu's concept of the 'ego-skin'.[3]

*Winnicott and Paradox*

'By ego-skin I mean a figuration used by the child's ego during early phases in his development to represent himself to himself as I, as ego, on the basis of his experience of the surface of the body. This corresponds to the moment at which the psychical ego is differentiated from the corporal ego at the operative level and remains confused with it at the figurative level.'[3]

D. Anzieu thinks that

'the ego-skin is supported by three functions of the skin. In its first function, the skin is that which contains inside the good and the full that suckling, maternal care, being constantly talked to by the mother, have built up in it. In its second function, the skin is the surface that marks the limit with the outside and keeps the outside outside, it is the barrier that protects from aggression coming from others, whether persons or objects. Lastly, in its third function, the skin, at the same time as the mouth, and at least as much as it, is a locus and a primary means of exchange with others.'

As we saw on *Figure 1(a)*, through an active adapting to the child's needs, the environment allows him to live in peaceful isolation. The infant does not know this. In that state, he makes a spontaneous movement that allows the discovery of the environment without the sense of the self being lost.

Motility and the gesture of what, in movement, is associated with the biological appear in the movement performed to reach the object in the outside world. The response of the object will offer a kind of anchorage, thus producing two linked circles (*Figure 1(b)* and *(c)*). Faulty adaptation on the part of the child

**Figure 3**
**Theoretical first feed**

Environment

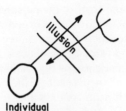

Individual
*Source*: Winnicott (1975)

**Figure 4**
**Positive value of illusion. The first possession = transitional object**

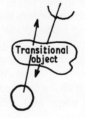

28

results in an impingement of the environment, so that the individual must become a reactor to this impingement (*Figure 2(b)*). In this situation, the sense of self is lost and is only regained by a return to isolation. (Note the introduction of the *time factor*, which indicates that a *process* is in progress.)

In *Figure 3*, which illustrates a theoretical first feed, we see how 'the creative potential of the individual arising out of need produces readiness for an hallucination'. The mother's close identification with her infant 'makes her aware of the infant's needs to the extent that she provides something more or less in the right place at the right time. This, much repeated, starts off the inability to use *illusion*, without which no contact is possible between the psyche and the environment.' We shall see later how transitional object and transitional phenomenon occur in this area,

> 'this intermediate area of illusion which in infancy is an agreed area, unchallenged in respect of its being created by the infant or accepted as a bit of perceived reality. We allow the infant this madness, and only gradually ask for a clear distinguishing between the subjective and that which is capable of objective or scientific proof. We adults use the arts and religion for the off-moments which we all need in the course of reality-testing and reality-acceptance.'

In an environment that 'holds' the baby sufficiently well, the baby is capable of undergoing personal development on the basis of inherited tendencies. A continuity of life then results that becomes in the end a sense of existing, a sense of self, leading ultimately to autonomy.

The mother who has sufficient 'adequation' towards her baby and who is not herself sick will allow the infant to evolve towards maturation and independence. The aetiology of the psychoses is almost always bound up with 'a failure in the total infant-care process'.[4]

INTEGRATION

'The keyword is integration which leads the baby to a state of unity, to the personal pronoun "I", to the number one; it makes possible the "I am" that gives a sense to "I do".'

The term 'personalization', a sort of positive form of 'depersonalization', implies that the developing infant or patient loses contact with his baby and his bodily functions, which implies the existence of some other aspects of the personality. The healthy child 'can use relationships in which there is maximum trust, and in such a relationship can at times disintegrate, depersonalize and even for a moment abandon the almost fundamental urge to exist and to feel existent'. The two things go together in healthy development, facilitating 'in-dwelling or the inhabitation of the body and the body functioning'.

### Artistic expression

'It is sometimes assumed that in health the individual is always integrated, as well as living in his own body, and able to feel that the world is real. There is, however, much sanity that has a symptomatic quality, being charged with fear or denial of madness, fear or denial of the innate capacity of every human being to become unintegrated, depersonalized, and to feel that the world is unreal. Sufficient lack of sleep produces these conditions in anyone. Through artistic expression we can hope to keep in touch with our primitive selves whence the most intense feelings and even fearfully acute sensations derive, and we are poor indeed if we are only sane.'[5]

### Childhood's imaginary companions

'A problem related to that of personalization is that of the imaginary companions of childhood. These are not simple fantasy constructions. Study of the future of these imaginary companions (in analysis) shows that they are sometimes other selves of a highly primitive type. . . . This very primitive and magical creation of imaginary companions is easily used as a defence, as it magically by-passes all the anxieties associated with incorporation, digestion, retention, and expulsion.'

In the developing human being integration takes many different forms. One of these is the establishment of a satisfactory modus vivendi between the psyche and the soma. This modus vivendi begins to be established before the time when it becomes necessary to take account of the concepts of intellect and verbalization.

The basis of a self is fashioned on the existence of the body, which, because it is alive, not only has a form, but also functions.

The dwelling in the body of this other part of the personality, linked with the psyche, represents from the developmental point of view a stage crossed in the way to health. Thus an infant who suffers from some deformity will not necessarily have a deformed self, providing he has the sense that he is a person accepted as a person. We have seen how a mother constantly presents her child with his body and psyche. This easy, but important task 'becomes difficult if the infant has some anomaly of which the mother is ashamed, for which she feels guilty, which frightens her, makes her impatient, or desperate'. And Winnicott adds: 'All she can do is to do her best; nothing more.'

Winnicott cites the case[6] of a boy suffering from syndactyly. He had had to adapt to the attitude of his mother and other people to his deformity, that is to say, in the end, he saw himself as abnormal. At first, however, for the child, normality is the shape of his body and his bodily functions: he must be accepted as such, he must be loved as such, without prior condition.

The part of the infant's development called *personalization* may be described as the dwelling of the psyche in the body; it has its roots in the mother's ability to add her emotional commitment to a commitment that, in origin, is physical and physiological.

A seventeen-year-old girl[7] has problems at school: for instance, when she is writing an essay, she can't get beyond a certain point. During the consultation, she says that her left leg is half an inch shorter than her right leg: this certainly isn't visible, but it obviously is very important to her. She dreams that she has a leg missing. Winnicott returns to her inability to concentrate and says that it was as if she felt that there would be something missing – like with her essays – if all the parts of her person were brought together to see how it made up a whole. Her father died when she was three and she had had to live with this unavoidable fact. Winnicott relates the child's reaction to her father's death, 'when a part of her life died with him in such a way that he had something missing'. Given the fact that, in the consultation, it had emerged that she placed great importance on her teeth, he added that one might say that 'she had bitten something off her father'. Many young children play with their fathers' fingers or with anything else that belongs to him and start biting it. In the present case, the death and disappearance of the father could therefore be felt as if she had actually bitten him and not as if she had merely been playing at biting. 'This led to a fantasy concerned with the amputation of a finger.' And Winnicott concludes that the central theme was her sense that, if she were examined, one would always find something missing: 'As it happened, the amputated limb was the left leg, her shorter leg.'

## AMBIVALENCE AND CONCERN

Setting out with the complex processes of maturation, Winnicott chose among the many stages described by Freud and later psychoanalysts one that involves the use of the term 'fusion'. This refers to the culmination of emotional development during which the young child feels erotic and aggressive impulses towards the same object at the same time. As far as eroticism is concerned, there is a seeking after satisfaction and an object, and, in the case of aggressiveness, a mixture of anger involving muscular eroticism and hatred, which implies that, by way of comparison, a good object image is maintained. In all aggressive, destructive impulses, there is also a primitive type of object-relation in which love involves destruction. The young child who has become capable of linking erotic and aggressive experience in a relationship with a single object achieves ambivalence.

Before ambivalence has become a fact in the child's development, the infant must have had the experience of ambivalence in fantasy and in his bodily functions, for fantasy is, originally, an elaboration. The infant also begins to establish relationships with objects that are less and less subjective phenomena and more and more perceived objectively as 'non-ego' elements.[8] He has begun to establish a 'self', a unit, that is, as we have seen, both physically contained within the skin and psychologically integrated. The mother has now become – in the child's mind – a coherent image that may be designated as a 'total object'. The child has succeeded in becoming integrated: he has become a complete thing emerging from the 'environment-individual set-up', like Humpty Dumpty perched on a wall instead of being 'devotedly held'. As far as his emotional development is concerned, his situation is precarious and particularly susceptible to irreversible disintegration.

This evolution implies an ego that is beginning to be independent of the mother's auxiliary ego; it may now be said that the infant has an inside and, consequently, an outside. The bodily schema has begun to exist and rapidly develops in a complex way. From then on, the infant lives a psychosomatic life. The inner psychical reality, which Freud has taught us to respect, now becomes a real thing for the infant, who experiences the sense that personal richness dwells inside the self. This personal richness is developed out of the simultaneous experience of love and hate, which implies the successful acquisition of ambivalence. The enrichment and refinement of this ambivalence will lead to the appearance of concern.

According to Winnicott's theory, concern appears in the life of the young child as a highly elaborate experience during the encounter, in the child's mind, of the object-mother and the environment-mother. The infant feels anxiety because he will lose his mother if he devours her; however, this anxiety is modified by the fact that he has a contribution to make to the environment-mother. He becomes more and more certain that he will be given opportunities of contributing an element to the mother-environment, of offering her something, and this certainty makes him capable of containing his anxiety. Anxiety contained in this way is transformed qualitatively and becomes a sense of guilt.

Id-impulses lead to a ruthless use of objects, and therefore to a sense of *guilt*, which is contained and appeased by what the infant is able to give the environment-mother at certain times. Furthermore, the opportunities of giving and making *reparation*, which the environment-mother provides by her regular presence, enables the infant to experience his id-impulses more and more boldly and, in other words, free him from instinctual life.

33

Thus guilt is not felt; it remains dormant or *in potentia* and appears (as sadness or depression) only if the opportunity to make reparation is lacking.[9]

When trust has been established, when the favourable cycle described above is repeated, and when opportunities present themselves, guilt concerning the id-impulses alters again. It is then that we need a more positive term such as 'concern'. The infant is now capable of feeling involved, of assuming responsibility for his own id-impulses and for the functions associated with them. This provides one of the fundamental, constructive elements of both play and work.

It should be observed that although all that is good or bad in the child's environment is not in fact a projection, it is paradoxically indispensable for his normal development that everything should appear to him as a projection. What we have here is omnipotence and the pleasure principle in action.

In analysis, interpretations that bring about changes are those given in terms of projection. The same goes for those factors that have aroused satisfaction: they will be interpreted in terms of the individual's love and of its ambivalence.

## From inner reality to outer reality

INNER REALITY AND CONFLICT: 'THE OBSERVATION OF INFANTS IN A SET SITUATION'

Though faithful to his medical and paediatric origins, Winnicott remained a psychoanalyst and psychotherapist on both the theoretical and clinical planes. Though, generally speaking, his work is based on a reconstruction of psychotic and anti-social cases, his observations of the early relationships between the mother and her child, which he relates in this article, make it of crucial importance in an understanding of that work.

Thus he has shown that, for him, hesitation, a sign of anxiety in the situation that he describes during an objective observation, indicates the existence of a superego in the child's mind: the child's behaviour cannot be explained without the hypothesis of infantile fantasy.

The setting is his office at Paddington Green Children's

Hospital, to which mothers could bring their children without appointment. This office is a large room, because so much can be seen and done in the time that it takes the mother and her child to reach the therapist from the door at the opposite end of the room. By the time the mother has reached him he has made contact with her and probably with the child.

If it was an infant, he asked the mother to sit opposite him with the angle of the table coming between him and her. She would sit down with the baby on her knee. As a matter of routine, he placed a right-angled shining spatula at the edge of the table and asked the mother to place the child in such a way that, if the child wanted to handle the spatula, it could do so. Usually, mothers showed by their ability or relative inability to follow this suggestion something of their personality.

So the child was on mother's knee, with a new person (a man, as it happened) sitting opposite, and there was a shining spatula on the table. (If visitors attended the consultation, they were asked to remain neutral.)

The baby is inevitably attracted by the shiny metal object. During the first stage, the baby usually puts out his hand to the spatula, then discovers that the situation merits reflexion, or, with his hand on the spatula and his body motionless, he looks first at Winnicott, then at his mother, with wide-opened eyes, waiting to judge their reaction; alternatively, he loses all interest and buries his face in his mother's bosom. The baby's gradual, spontaneous revival of interest in the spatula is curious to observe. While the 'period of hesitation' lasts, the baby holds his body still, but not rigid. During the second stage, however, the picture changes fairly quickly.

'The child's acceptance of the reality of desire for the spatula is heralded by a change in the inside of the mouth, which becomes flabby, while the tongue looks thick and soft and saliva flows copiously. Before long he puts the spatula into his mouth and is chewing it with his gums. . . . Instead of expectancy and stillness there now develops self-confidence, and there is free bodily movement. . . . The baby now seems to feel that the spatula is in his possession, perhaps in his power, certainly available for the purposes of self-expression.

35

He bangs with it on the table or on a metal bowl which is nearby on the table, making as much noise as he can; or else he holds it to his mouth and to his mother's mouth, very pleased if we *pretend* to be fed by it. He definitely wishes us to *play* at being fed and is upset if we should be so stupid as to take the thing into our mouths and spoil the game as a game.'[10]

A third phase appears: the baby first drops the spatula as if by mistake. If it is given back to him, he is pleased, plays with it again, and drops it once more, but this time, less by mistake – this is repeated a few times and the baby is especially pleased when it makes a ringing sound on contact with the floor. This third phase comes to an end when the baby wants to get down on to the floor with the spatula, where he starts putting it into his mouth and playing with it again, or else gets bored with it and reaches out to any other objects that lie at hand.

'It now seems to me', says Winnicott,' that my observations could be looked at as an extension backwards of this particular observation of Freud's.[11] I think the cotton-reel, standing for the child's mother, is thrown away to indicate a getting rid of the mother because the reel in his possession has represented the mother *in his possession*. . . . I now see the throwing-away of the cotton-reel as a part of a game, the rest being implied, or played at an earlier stage. In other words, when the mother goes away, this is not only a loss for him of the externally real mother, but also a test of the child's relation to his *inside* mother.'

This inside mother to a large extent reflects his own feelings and may be loving or terrifying, or switch rapidly from one to the other. When he finds he can master his relation to his inside mother, including his aggressive riddance of her, 'he can allow the disappearance of his external mother, and not too greatly fear her return'. Then he adds: 'The loss of the internal mother, who had acquired for the infant the significance of an inner source of love and protection and of life itself, greatly strengthens the threat of loss of the actual mother.' By throwing away the spatula or cotton-reel, the infant 'does not only get rid of an external and internal mother . . . He also externalizes an internal mother whose loss is feared, so as to demonstrate to himself that this internal mother, now represented through the toy on the floor, has not vanished from his inner world, has not been destroyed by the act of incorporation, is still friendly and willing to be played with. And by all this the child revises his relations with things and people both inside and outside himself.'

Thus the child gains relief from the depressed mood that accompanies anxiety about the internal mother and happiness is regained.

The practical description that he makes of his observation is valid, he says, for infants between five and thirteen months approximately; beyond that age, the child's positive interest becomes too extensive to be assessed in this way.

Winnicott never loses sight of the possible therapeutic work in this set situation. He provides a few examples.

A baby girl who had attended from six to eight months on account of feeding disturbance, presumably initiated by infective gastro-enteritis. The child's emotional development was upset by this illness. All play ceased, and by nine months not only was the infant's relation to people entirely unsatisfactory, but she also began to have fits. At twelve months the baby was having major fits followed by sleepiness. At this stage Winnicott started seeing her every few days and giving her twenty minutes' personal attention, in the set situation described above, but with the infant on his own knee. At one consultation she made a furtive attempt to bite Winnicott's knuckles. Three days later he had her again on his knees and she bit his knuckles so severely that the skin was nearly torn. She then played at throwing spatulas on the floor incessantly for fifteen minutes. All the time she cried as if really unhappy. Two days later after four convulsions in the previous two days, she spent half an hour on Winnicott's knees: she cried as usual, bit his knuckles very severely, this time without showing guilt feelings, and then played the game of biting and throwing away spatulas. While on his knee she became able to enjoy play. After a time she began to finger her toes. Later the mother came and said that since the last consultation the baby had been 'a different child'. She had not only had no fits, but had been sleeping well at night and been happy all day.

Good clinician that he was, Winnicott noticed that the fluidity of the infant's personality and the fact that feelings and unconscious processes are so close to the early stages of babyhood make it possible for changes to be brought about in the course of a few interviews. This fluidity, however, must also mean that the infant is still liable to neurosis at a later stage; however, it is a good prognostic sign if a child's first year goes well.

As Freud (1926) said, 'anxiety is *about* something'. There are two things, to discuss: the things that happen in the body and mind in a state of anxiety, and the something that there is anxiety about. Using the set situation and technique on a child who was regularly observed, Winnicott realized that this child's asthma was connected with a certain category of feelings and that, in a series of familial events, this asthma was connected with a clearly defined stage.

Margaret, a seven-month-old girl, is brought by her mother because the night before the consultation she has been breathing wheezily all night. Otherwise she is a very happy child who sleeps well and takes food well. Her relations with both parents are good, especially with her father, a night worker, who sees a lot of her. She already says 'Dad-dad', but not 'Ma-ma'. She goes to her father when she doesn't feel well and he manages to get her to sleep. There is a sister two years older. The mother explains that she herself developed asthma when she became pregnant with this one. The little girl's asthma did not come entirely unheralded. The mother reports that for three days Margaret has been stirring in her sleep, only sleeping ten minutes at a time, waking with screaming and trembling. For a month, she has been putting her fists to her mouth and this has recently become somewhat compulsive and anxious. For three days she has had a slight cough but the wheeziness only became definite the night before the consultation. Here are Winnicott's detailed notes taken at the time:

'I stood up a right-angled spatula on the table and the child was immediately interested, looked at it, looked at me, and gave me a long look with big eyes and sighs. For five minutes this continued, the child being unable to make up her mind to take the spatula. When at length she took it, she was at first unable to make up her mind to put it in her mouth, although she quite clearly wanted to do so. After a time she found she was able to take it, as if gradually getting reassured from our staying as we were. On her taking it to herself I noted the usual flow of saliva, and then followed several minutes of enjoyment of the mouth experience. It will be noted that this behaviour corresponded to what I call the normal.'

In the second consultation Margaret reached out to take the spatula, but again hesitated, exactly as at the first visit, and again only gradually became able to mouth and to enjoy the spatula with confidence. She was more eager in her mouthing of it than she had been at the previous occasion, and made noises while chewing it. She soon dropped it deliberately and on its being returned played with it with excitement and noise, obviously pleased, and kicking out. There was a bowl there, too, but it was only after a while that the infant brought the two objects together, making a noise on the bowl with the spatula. This illustrated her difficulty, as well as her growing ability regarding the management of *two people*. When, exactly, did she have an asthma attack?

'The baby sat on her mother's lap with the table between them and me [Winnicott recounts]. The mother held the child around the chest with her two hands supporting her body. It was therefore very easy to see when at a certain point the child developed bronchial spasm. The mother's hands indicated the exaggerated movement of the chest, both the deep inspiration and the prolonged obstructed expiration were shown up, and the noisy expiration could be heard. The mother could see as well as I did when the baby had asthma. *The asthma occurred on both occasions over the period in which the child hesitated about taking the spatula.* She put her hand to the spatula and then, as she controlled her body, her hand and her environment, she developed asthma, which involves an involuntary control of expiration. At the moment when she came to feel confident about the spatula which was at her mouth, when saliva flowed, when stillness changed to the enjoyment of activity and when watching changed into self-confidence, at this moment the asthma ceased.'

It was possible to see, because of the fact that the baby was being watched under known conditions, that for this child asthma was associated with the moment at which there is normally hesitation, and hesitation implies mental conflict.

'I suggest that the hesitation means that the infant *expects* to produce an angry and perhaps revengeful mother by his indulgence. In order that a baby shall feel threatened, even by a truly and obviously angry mother, he must have in his mind the notion of an angry mother. As Freud (1926) says: "On the other hand, the external (objective) danger must have managed to become internalized if it is to be significant for the ego."

'The "something" which the anxiety is about is in the infant's mind, an idea of potential evil or strictness, and into the novel situation anything that is in the infant's mind may be projected. When there has been no experience of prohibition, the hesitation implies conflict, or the existence in the baby's mind of a *fantasy* corresponding to the other baby's *memory* of his really strict mother. In either case, as a consequence, he has first to curb his interest and desire, and he only becomes able to find his desire again in so far as his testing of the environment affords satisfactory results.'

Winnicott supplied the setting for such a test. What, then, was that 'something' that the anxiety was about? Referring to the knowledge gained from the analysis of children between two and four years old, and to the works of Melanie Klein, Winnicott notes that 'one of the characteristics of a child at the age of two is that the primary oral fantasies, and the anxieties and defences belonging to them, are clearly discernible alongside secondary and highly elaborated mental processes.' In fact, for a seven-month-old infant, as in the case above, the fantasies were

'not yet attached to word-presentations, but they are full of content and rich in emotion, and it can be said that they provide the foundation on which all later fantasy life is built.'
'These fantasies of the infant are concerned not only with external environment, but also with the fate and inter-relationship of the people and bits of people that are being fantastically taken into him – at first along with his ingestion of food and subsequently as an independent procedure – and that builds up the inner reality.'

The qualities of good and bad depend on the relative acceptability of aim in the taking-in process. This in turn depends on the strength of the destructive impulses relative to the love impulses, and on the individual child's capacity to tolerate anxieties derived from destructive tendencies. Connected with both of these the nature of the child's defences has to be taken into account, including the degree of development of his capacity for making reparation. 'These things could be summed up by saying that the child's ability to keep alive what he loves and to retain his belief in his own love has an important bearing on how good or bad the things inside him and outside him feel to him to be.' As E. Martin[12] described it, the system of reparation in Winnicott is not comparable with that of Melanie Klein; in this system it may be said, roughly speaking, that if one eats something greedily, one will give it back and hurry to get it out again, and it will have to be restored as soon as possible, whereas with Winnicott, as he describes it on several occasions with his patients, there are blankets and cushions so that everybody can feel comfortable and the regression seem quite natural for the patient. Reparation occurs when the child feels predatory, that he is going to bite the breast, and that there is a 'hole', that he is going to be anxious, but what is described there is not a depressive position, but an anxiety for the object, a concern – there is no internal guilt. The time-factor will play a preponderant role since the mother must always appear both as she whose breast is eaten, and therefore who bears a hole, and she who continues to give her idyllic breasts. This time-factor allows the child to overcome his destructive impulses and, in this, Winnicott is very close to Freud. Winnicott writes,

'To the infant, so closely in touch with his mother's body and the contents of the breast, which she actually takes, the idea of reaching into the breast is by no means remote, and fear of reaching in to the inside of mother's body could easily be associated in the baby's mind with not breathing.'

At the sight of something particularly wonderful we sometimes say, 'It takes my breath away.'

The spatula may stand for the breast or perhaps for something that is more associated with the father than the mother and which the child will later come to know as the penis. However it also stands for people and especially for people's moods. Thus infants recognize people's habits and behave differently between one person and another. Thus Margaret turned easily towards her father and said: 'Dad-dad.' In another case related by Winnicott, a child played beside his mother as she was talking about a problem she was having with another child and, as he was playing, he suddenly looked up and asked: 'Dr Winnicott, are you tired?' The mother then explained that the father often came home tired and that the child felt this.

Extending his thinking to the ability to establish relationships involving two persons, Winnicott shows that in this situation the child may not have developed 'the capacity . . . for building up the whole person behind the part object', or has lost it. Either the spatula is for him merely an object, or he will show that he sees Winnicott or his mother behind the spatula, and behaves as if it were a part of himself (or of his mother). By taking or leaving the spatula, he alters the relationship of two people standing for father and mother. The infant, if he has the capacity to do so, finds himself dealing with two persons at once, mother and Winnicott. Many adult neurotics never succeed in managing a relation to two people at once and have got stuck at this primitive stage in infantile development. 'The conflict between love and hatred and the ensuing guilt and fear of losing what is loved, first experienced in relation to the mother only, is carried further into the infant's relation to both parents.' Thus in the case of Margaret, when the child becomes capable of bringing the spatula and the bowl together at the end of her game, we see the mixture of wishes and fears in regard to the management of a relation to two people at once.[13]

## Illusion and disillusionment

'An illusion is not the same thing as a mistake,' said Freud. 'It is not in fact necessarily a mistake . . . we call illusion a belief when the fulfilment of wishes is a primordial factor in its motivation.'

Winnicott illustrates illusion by an incident. One day, during a hot spell, an analyst had to do an extra analytic session in the lunch hour. He was tired and perhaps a little sleepy, and he had the following experience at the same time as being an ordinary competent analyst:

He could see out of his window, and on a roof some distance away he saw a man. This man was about forty-five years old and had a rather bald head. He had finished his sandwiches and had let his midday paper with its racing tips fall. Obviously he had allowed himself to drop off to sleep. Dimly aware of this the analyst would never have registered anything had it not been that there was a sequel. As we know, a continuous noise may be unnoticed until it stops. In this case the disturbing thing was that the man made no movement at all. After half an hour the analyst definitely registered the fact that the man ought to have woken up, and then suddenly the man's head swelled to the size of the rather large spherical stone ornament that it had been all the time. The sight of the man going to sleep had been no more than an indication that the analyst wanted to go to sleep himself.[14]

In 'Primitive Emotional Development',[15] Winnicott describes what he means by illusion from the angle of a 'good-enough' mother's double dependence. He observes,

'The baby has instinctual urges and predatory ideas. The mother has a breast and the power to produce milk, and the idea that she would like to be attacked by a hungry baby. These two phenomena do not come into relation with each other until the mother and child *live and experience together*.

'I think of the process as if two lines came from opposite directions, liable to come near each other. If they overlap there is a moment of *illusion* – a bit of experience which the infant can take as *either* his hallucination *or* a thing belonging to external reality.'

At first, a mere contact with external or shared reality is needed – the child hallucinating and the world offering – with moments of illusion for the child in which he regards the two aspects as identical, which in fact they never are. 'These ideas are enriched by actual details, sight, feel, smell, and next time this material is used in the hallucination.'

External reality imposes very real frustrations, but also bring relief and satisfaction. But in fantasy everything works by magic; 'there are no brakes on fantasy, and love and hate cause alarming effects. External reality has brakes on it, and can be studied and known, and, in fact, fantasy is only tolerable at full blast when objective reality is appreciated well.'

43

It will be seen that fantasy is not something that the individual creates in order to face the frustrations of external reality. This is true only of what Winnicott calls 'fantasying'. 'Fantasy is more primary than reality and the enrichment of fantasy with the world's riches depends on the experience of illusion.'

Illusion is a very large subject and provides the key to the child's interest in bubbles, clouds, rainbows, and all mysterious phenomena, and also to his interest in fluff. 'Somewhere here, too, is the interest in breath, which never decides whether it comes primarily from within or without, and which provides the basis for the conception of spirit, soul, *anima*.'

WEANING

Let us return to weaning and disillusionment. As we have seen, mental health is 'a product of the continuous care that enables a continuity of personal emotional growth'. It is the mother's devotion that forms the basis of mental health. In the article entitled 'Psychoses and Child Care',[16] which was addressed to physicians, Winnicott, taking the point of view of the psyche, while remaining a paediatrician, stresses that he is using this word 'to describe the essential feature without which the mother cannot make her contribution, a sensitive and active adaptation to her infant's needs – needs which at the beginning are absolute'. In his experience, when a child was 'difficult to wean', it was usually possible to detect disturbances in the mother, a difficulty in relation to the ambivalence of feelings, or a depressive tendency.[17]

Following on from his study of the psychoses, he notes that a healthy infant who 'has reached the age at which weaning is meaningful' has also acquired

> 'the capacity to become depressed (in the sense of showing a reactive depression or mood change). . . . The capacity to feel concern, to feel grief, and to react to loss in an organized way so that recovery may take place in the course of time, is a development stage of great importance in healthy growth.'

This capacity is laid down by the careful management of weaning, using weaning in the very broad sense.[18] As we have seen, to achieve normally the depressive position in emotional development presupposes an earlier healthy development.

The case of Louis[19] illustrates the development of the first year and the appearance at the moment of weaning of a symptom due to what may be regarded as 'an impingement of the environment'.

Louis, a five-month-old infant referred to a children's hospital in an almost cachectic state after feeding disturbances, had almost returned to his weight at birth in a few weeks. The departmental head had asked the psychiatrist to examine him. A nurse had drawn attention to a symptom: with serene face, his eyes opened, without any trace of discomfort or pain, Louis brought up part of the feed that he had absorbed several hours earlier. Was this a case of merycism? 'I went into the cubicle,' the doctor writes, 'where this baby was resting, and being fed by drip-feed. At once I was struck by Louis' gaze, which was all the more lively and alert because one could see only his dark eyes in his emaciated face. His expression was attentive, concentrated, observing the stranger that I was without either fear or pleasure, but with a sort of questioning. I was just as perplexed myself and wondered how I could make contact with a baby whom I could not take in my arms, because he was fixed to his perfusion board.'

He was the first-born of a young couple and the birth had taken place without difficulty, but the mother had gained 20 kg during her pregnancy without any alteration of appetite. After the birth, she easily reverted to her previous weight.

The parents worked in rotation, so that Louis was at home as much as possible. On the other hand, this system had the inconvenience for them that they crossed one another more than they were actually together. They got on well with the nurse, with no rivalry or dispute concerning the child's rearing. The only apparent problem had been the introduction of non-milk foods into the child's diet; the child soon showed his disapproval by refusing to feed throughout the day. The mother still felt very guilty about this attempt.

The anorexia and vomiting had appeared after a week spent entirely with both parents, who had taken advantage of holidays to take their baby away without any problem.

A number of points should be made.

Louis was present and took interest in the stimulations proposed: he reacted to the sound of a rattle, looked around him, grasped the light objects held out to him and brought them to his mouth. Wondering how he was to make contact with the child with a view to understanding what had led to such a state, the doctor 'began in a mechanical way to hum the tune of a cradle-song. Louis' eyes filled with tears, though none were shed; he managed to hold them back so that they did not trickle down his cheeks. Then he smiled, a very broad smile, and at the same time he brought up a little milk; that began again two or three times, gently, without any sudden expulsion, with a sort of joy, as if he had found only that way of communicating.'

The doctor discovered in a later interview that, at the beginning of the mother's pregnancy, a cancer had been discovered in *her* mother. Immediately after the birth, she had spent a complete month with her parents together with her husband and the newborn child. At the time, Louis was kept in a separate room, so as not to run the risk of tiring his grandmother. Doing everything possible to stop the baby crying too much, the parents were very soon struck by how good he was. He never demanded food; it was not until the episode of the first refusal to eat that it occurred to them that he might have a wilful, rebellious character.

'Immediately behind the weaning is the broader subject of disillusionment. If weaning implies a successful feeding, disillusion implies that the opportunity to have illusions is being given.' The earlier stages in emotional development will be elucidated mainly in the psychoanalyst's office, for 'psychoanalysis is far from being the most precise of instruments', but there could be room within its framework 'for an infinite variety of experiences'. Furthermore, one also has at one's disposal work in the field of direct observation.[20]

So, on the basis of the unit formed by the 'environment–individual' set-up, the environment created by the individual begins to look, if all goes well, like the one that is usually seen; the process of development then reaches a stage that allows the individual to pass from the stage of dependence to that of independence. This hazardous period is one when mental health is built up and psychosis avoided if it is successfully passed through.

TOWARDS INDEPENDENCE

By *constantly* providing the child with 'the simplified bit of the world' that he is able to know through her, the mother gives him the foundations on which objectivity or a scientific attitude are built. 'It is on the basis of monotony that a mother may succeed in enriching her child's world.' As a result, it is possible to remedy something. The mother's technique allows the love and hate that coexist in the child to be distinguished, to establish their relations, and gradually to succeed in being mastered in a healthy way.[21] It makes it possible to elaborate the consequences of instinctual experiences; this elaboration is similar to the digestive process, which is of equivalent complexity.

We should also recall the story of the Piggle: sometimes her mother has to fall and hurt herself and then Piggle does things to make her better. This again shows, if there were any need to do so, that love and hate for the mother appear simultaneously and that Piggle is quite capable of using her mother in an aggressive way. The therapist's hypothesis is that, for this child, the 'black mummy' meant that hate (or dis-illusion) had made its appearance.

Thus it is not possible for the infant to move from the pleasure principle to the reality principle, or to go towards primary identification and beyond, outside the presence of a good enough mother, a mother who is able to adapt in an active, unconstraining, and unresentful way. In time, this adaptation is felt less and less in terms of the growing ability acquired by the child to confront maternal failure. In 'Transitional Objects and Transitional Phenomena', Winnicott reminds us of the infant's means of dealing with this maternal failure:

1. The infant's experience, often repeated, that there is a time limit to frustration. At first, naturally, this time limit must be short.
2. A growing sense of process.
3. The beginnings of mental activity.
4. The employment of auto-erotic satisfactions.
5. Remembering, re-living, fantasying, dreaming; the integration of past, present, and future.

*If all goes well* the infant can actually come to gain from the experience of frustration, since incomplete adaptation to need makes objects real, that is to say, hated as well as loved. The consequence of this is that *if all goes well* the infant can be

47

disturbed by a close adaptation to need that is continued too long, not allowed its natural decrease, since exact adaptation resembles magic and the object that behaves perfectly becomes no better than an hallucination.[23] At the beginning omnipotence is almost a fact of experience. The mother's eventual task is gradually to disillusion the infant, but she has no hope of success unless at first she has been able to give sufficient opportunity for illusion.

'In another language, the breast is created by the infant over and over again out of the infant's capacity to love or (one can say) out of need.' A subjective phenomenon develops in the baby that we call the mother's breast – by which, Winnicott adds, he includes the whole technique of mothering. 'The mother places the actual breast just there where the infant is ready to create, and at the right moment.' There is no exchange between the mother and the infant.[23]

From birth, therefore, the human being is concerned with the problem of the relationship between what is objectively perceived and what is subjectively conceived of. In the solution of this problem there is no health for the human being who has not been started off well enough by the mother. The intermediate area to which Winnicott refers is 'situated between primary creativity and objective perception based on reality-testing'.

The transitional phenomena represent the early stages of the use of illusion, without which there is no meaning for the human being in the idea of a relationship with an object that is perceived by others as external to that being. For Winnicott, the question of illusion is inherent in the human condition and no individual would ever succeed in solving it for himself, though a *theoretical* understanding of the problem may provide a *theoretical* solution. If the disillusionment process goes well, the stage is set for the frustrations that we gather together under the word weaning.

If the illusion-disillusionment process goes astray the infant cannot attain to so normal a thing as weaning, nor to a reaction to weaning, and it is then absurd to refer to weaning at all. The mere termination of breast-feeding is not a weaning.

On the subject of the illusion-disillusionment theory, Winnicott considers that the task of reality-acceptance is never completed; no human being is free from the strain of relating inner and outer reality. Nevertheless, an unchallenged intermediate area of experience in direct continuity with the play area of the small child who is 'lost' in play is one that we all know as adults: that of the arts, religion, etc.

# 3  Fear of breakdown

In an article written shortly before his death, called 'Fear of Breakdown',[1] Winnicott considers a type of anxiety frequently seen in certain patients and which they rationalize in the form of: 'I'm afraid I'm going to have a breakdown.'

Several clinical and theoretical problems are dealt with in this article. The paradox of Winnicott's observation is to attribute this fear not to an anxiety projected into the future, but to an earlier experience on the part of the individual. In fact it is not a depression that might occur, but a depression that has already taken place, long ago. We are confronted here with a failure of a defensive organization: 'It is the ego organization that is threatened. But the ego cannot organize against environmental failure in so far as dependence is a living fact.'[2]

Before examining more fully a concept that Winnicott did not have time to elaborate as much as he might have wished, we must return to another paradoxical situation, that of *primary maternal preoccupation*,[3] that is to say, 'a very special state of the mother', which gradually develops during pregnancy, lasts for several weeks after the birth, and which mothers find it difficult to remember. This 'organized state' may be compared with a withdrawn state or even with a schizoid episode. 'I bring in the word "illness" because a woman must be healthy in order both to develop this state and to recover from it as the infant releases her.' This is implied in the term 'devoted' in Winnicott's expression 'ordinary devoted mother'. This special state of a normal mother and her cure have a corollary in the child. The infant has

(a) a constitution;
(b) innate development tendencies ('conflict-free area in ego');
(c) motility and sensitivity;
(d) instincts, themselves involved in the developmental tendency, with changing zone-dominance.

As we have seen, if the mother provides a good enough adaptation to needs, the child's line of life is very little disturbed by reactions to the impingement of the environment. Maternal failures produce phases of reaction to impingement and these reactions interrupt the 'going on being' of the infant. 'An excess of this reacting produces not frustration, but a *threat of annihilation*. This in my view is a very real primitive anxiety, long antedating any anxiety that includes the word death in its description.' It follows that any failure on the part of the mother during the earliest phase in the infant's life is a threat to personal self-existence.

The early building up of the ego is therefore silent.

'The first ego organization comes from the experiencing of threats of annihilation which do not lead to annihilation and from which, repeatedly, there is *recovery*. Out of such experiences, confidence in recovery begins to be something which leads to an ego and to an ego capacity for coping with frustration. . . . At the beginning the failing mother is not apprehended as such. Indeed a recognition of absolute dependence on the mother and of her capacity for primary maternal preoccupation, or whatever it is called, is something which belongs to *extreme sophistication*, and to a stage not always reached by adults.'

'Without the initial good-enough environmental provision this self that can afford to die never develops. The feeling of real is absent and if there is not too much chaos the ultimate feeling is of futility. . . . If there is not chaos, there appears a false self that hides the true self, that complies with demands, that reacts to stimuli, that rids itself of instinctual experiences by having them, but that is only playing for time.'

To sum up, in the earlier stages of emotional development, when the process of maturation is innate, the individual passes from absolute dependence, or 'double-dependence', to relative independence and is on the road to independence. In a healthy individual, the development takes place at a pace that does not exceed that of the development of complexity in the mental mechanisms – this development being itself bound up with neuro-physiological development. As we have seen, the facilitating environment may be described as providing the holding, the cares or handling, to which the presentation of the object is added. In such an environment, the individual passes through a development that may be classified into various categories: *integration*, indwelling (or *psychosomatic collusion*), and object relationship. Thus this forward movement in development may be paralleled with the threat and defences against that threat of a retrograde movement in schizophrenia.

Winnicott's main theme is that the clinical fear of breakdown is fear of a breakdown that has already been experienced. It is fear of that original agony that has caused the defensive organization that the patient manifests in the form of a syndrome of illness. Sometimes this syndrome appears only after important progress has been made in treatment. Thus dependence does not become part of the transference at once.

To understand what Winnicott means by this fear of breakdown, let us take what he describes as 'the primitive agonies'. He lists some of these:

(a) a return to an unintegrated state (defence: disintegration);
(b) falling for ever (defence: self-holding);
(c) loss of psychosomatic collusion, the failure of 'indwelling' (defence: depersonalization);[4]
(d) loss of sense of real (defence: exploitation of primary narcissism, etc.);
(e) loss of capacity to relate to objects (defence: autistic states, relating only to self-phenomena).[5]

Winnicott stresses that it is a mistake to regard psychotic illness as a breakdown for, he says, 'it is a defence organization relative to a primitive agony, usually successful (except when the facilitating environment has been not deficient but tantalizing, perhaps the worst thing that can happen to a human baby'.

Winnicott never failed to acknowledge his debt to his patients, who were the inspiration behind most of his concepts. 'It is to one of them that I owe the term "phenomenal death".'[6]

How can the clinician use this idea? 'We cannot hurry up our patients. Nevertheless, we can hold up their progress because of genuinely not knowing; any little piece of our understanding may help us to keep up with a patient's needs.' This fact that the patient carries hidden in the unconscious (unconscious, in the particular context referred to by Winnicott) 'means that the ego integration is not able to encompass something. The ego is too immature to gather all the phenomena into the area of personal omnipotence.'

What happens, then, in treatment? 'The original experience of primitive agony cannot get into the past tense unless the ego can first gather it into its own present time and experience omnipotent control now (assuming the auxiliary ego-supporting function of the mother [analyst]).'

How can one 'remember' a breakdown that has already taken place and which is situated shortly after the individual begins his life? The only way in this case is for the patient to have – in the transference – for the first time the experience of this past thing. This past and future thing then becomes a question of 'here and now'. It is the equivalent of *recall* and this culmination is equivalent to the lifting of repression that occurs in the analysis of the neurotic (in classical Freudian analysis).

Winnicott links this concept to the fear of death. Quoting Keats's words 'half in love with easeful death' and longing for the ease that would come if he could 'remember' having died, he emphasizes that he must therefore feel the experience of death now.

'Many men and women spend their lives wondering whether to find a solution by suicide, that is, sending the body to death which has already happened to the psyche. Suicide is no answer, however, but is a despair gesture. I now understand for the first time what my schizophrenic patient (who did kill herself) meant when she said: "All I ask you to do is to help me to commit suicide for the right reason instead of for the wrong reason." I did not succeed, and she killed herself in despair of finding the solution. Her aim (as I now see) was to get it stated by me that she died in early infancy. On this basis, I think she and I could have enabled her to put off body death till old age took its toll.'

In the case of this patient, the disturbance began very early, for there had been a premature awareness before birth as a result of the mother's panic, and, furthermore, the birth was complicated by an undiagnosed *placenta praevia*.[7]

Thus the patient was not mature enough to experience the sense of annihilation: a schema had developed in which continuity of being was interrupted by the patient's infantile reactions to impingement, that is to say, to factors coming from the environment, which the patient, because of her weaknesses, allowed to intrude into her development.

In practice, the difficulty lies in the fact that the patient fears the terrifying nature of the void and will organize, in order to defend himself, a controlled void, for example, by not eating (anorexia nervosa), or by refusing to learn (intellectual inhibition), or again he will constantly fill himself in compulsive bulimia. But if the experience of the void has not been experienced as such at the beginning, it then becomes fear that is nevertheless compulsively sought.

There may be a positive element in this, that is to say the fact that 'only out of non-existence can existence start'

'The individual cannot develop from an ego root if this is divorced from psychosomatic experience and primary narcissism. It is just here that begins the intellectualization of the ego-functions. It can be noted here that all this is a long distance in time prior to the establishment of anything that could usefully be called the self.'[8]

As J.-B. Pontalis very judiciously remarks in his Preface to the French Edition of *Playing and Reality*, 'the central paradox' is that the breakdown 'takes place without finding its psychical locus' and is laid nowhere. He stresses the importance of the void, of the negative in Winnicott, concepts that have also been stressed in England by Marion Milner (the empty space) and in France by André Green (negative hallucination and the theme of the absent).

J.-B. Pontalis goes on to write: 'The unthinkable makes the thought. What has not been lived, experienced, what eludes any possible recall is at the heart of *being*' – and he stresses the introduction of this word into psychoanalysis.[9]

# 4 The self and communication

From his student days, as we have seen, Winnicott was a man of his times. His concepts and his techniques were based on his many-faceted experience – in particular his experience of mothers and infants in paediatrics and of psychoanalysis in his practice. His contributions as consultant, teacher, or lecturer reveal his very personal approach, practice, and theory enriching one another. We shall now examine some of his notions, only too well aware that we cannot tackle all of them. We shall begin with those that were more directly inspired by his work as a consultant psychiatrist for the National Evacuation Plan during World War II.[1]

## The Anti-Social Tendency[2]

Winnicott strove to understand and to confront anti-social behaviour in the normal or almost normal child in terms of deprivation and in relation to hope.

If *privation* is related to the failure of the environment that took place at the stage of absolute dependence, when the infant had no way of apprehending maternal care, *deprivation* implies that there was a loss of something good. 'When he steals an object, the child is looking for the capacity to find, he is not looking for

56

an object.'³ Thus, as we can see in *Therapeutic Consultations in Child Psychology*,⁴ when the anti-social tendency is the major symptom presented by the child, whether he steals and demands special attention from his mother by his behaviour, etc., or whether he is calling through his destructive acts for energetic measures, but without reprisals, the anamnesis usually reveals that 'the environment enabled the child to make a good start', but then some environmental lapse led to the blockage of the maturational process. The child may then identify with the environment and lose his own spontaneity, being unable to bear any situation in which he has to face up to his aggressiveness. *From the child's point of view*, there is now a gap between this environmental failure and whatever there may be in the way of recovery. Such a child 'is most of the time hopeless, hopeless because of the break in the continuity of his or her life-line, the break being due to a massive reaction in the child, automatic and inevitable, to an environmental failure'. However, what the child feels as deprivation will not necessarily be perceived as such by the parents.⁵

'In so far as there is recovery the child can be said to be (a) most of the time in a somewhat depressed state, hopeless, but not knowing why, and then (b) the child begins to get hope. There is hope perhaps because of something good happening in the environment.' Communication may prove to be the only thing necessary for the child to become hopeful once more, to rediscover 'the lost object or the lost maternal provision, or the lost family structure.'

## On communication

Winnicott often comes back to communication. In his 'Communicating and Not Communicating',⁶ he reminds us that at the earliest stages of emotional development, silent communication concerns the subjective aspect of objects. This is close to what Freud said of psychical reality and of the unconscious that can never be conscious, and of what Melanie Klein says about internal experiences. For 'internal' cannot be used in this sense, he goes on, since the infant has not yet established a defined frontier for the ego. The good-enough initial environment provides the continuous sense of existing on which the ego is built. 'There is no id before ego':[7] phenomena have to be 'covered and catalogued and experienced and eventually interpreted by ego-functioning'. The ego is prior to the self, which 'arrives after the child has begun to use the intellect to look at what others see or feel or hear, and what they conceive of when they meet this infant body'.

## The self, something alive

*Figures* 5, 6, and 7 in 'Psychoses and Child Care'[8] illustrate the place of primary madness and the split in the 'environment–individual' set-up resulting from a failure in active adaptation on the part of the environment in the early stages of life. If the split is too great, the secret inner life has very little in it derived from external reality and is truly incommunicable. There is a

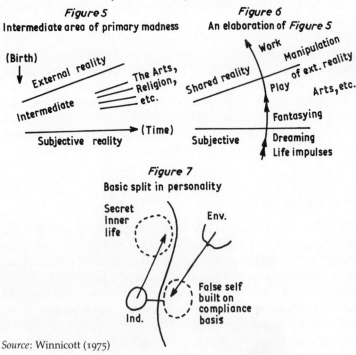

**Figure 5**
Intermediate area of primary madness

**Figure 6**
An elaboration of *Figure 5*

**Figure 7**
Basic split in personality

*Source*: Winnicott (1975)

great danger for the individual of being seduced into a false life and the instincts then come in on the side of the seducing environment. We shall now try to examine this process in terms of two articles each of which throws light on the other: 'Mind and Its Relation to the Psyche-soma' (1949)[9] and 'Ego Distortion in Terms of True and False Self' (1960).[10]

The split between true self and false self occurs in all individuals to varying degrees. The good-enough mother responds to the infant's omnipotence, and to some extent, gives it a meaning: a true self then begins to come to life. If she is not good enough, instead of responding to his gesture she substitutes for it her own, which will have meaning only through the infant's submission. This is the earliest stage of the false self.

MIND AND PSYCHE-SOMA

His work with pre-psychotic children and his experience of borderline cases in particular led Winnicott to consider the psyche-soma set-up: the psyche, which includes the sense of self that will be *the* self and the *soma qua* perception of the body. This psyche-soma set-up, when everything goes well, will therefore be the basis of a good self, given a good-enough mother, gradual disillusion, etc. Another element, which he calls 'mind', now comes into play. In this earliest development of the individual, health goes hand in hand with continuity of existence. If the mother's activity is not manifested in the right place at the right time, by responding to the infant's spontaneous gestures or sensorial hallucination,[11] a false self is set up and the child is subjected to external impingements. It may also happen that the child's state of excitement is too great and that the mother is unable to express her aggression and bear it. There then occurs the possibility of control continued by the activity of the mind, which will be able to induce a precocious hyper-maturation of the processes of knowledge.[12]

'I don't think the mind really exists as an entity,' wrote Ernest Jones (1936).

The bodily schema with its aspects relating to time and space provide a valuable description of an individual's representation of himself. The psyche derives directly from the soma; thus a

59

*Winnicott and Paradox*

hole is formed at once that is situated in what Winnicott describes at the heart of the dependence system. At first sensations will be felt necessarily, by definition, in the body, and the first self-knowledge will be a kind of continuity of life, which is therefore experienced, it would seem, in a diffused, vague way, but in the form of care, elementary sensations, gradually synthesized noises in something. At a given moment, therefore, needs will actually occur. Now the satisfaction of needs is not, Winnicott notes, the satisfaction of instincts, for, at this period, instincts are not yet clearly defined and moves towards a state in which instinctual needs will be felt as forming part of the self and of the environment. When the mother is good enough, everything will come together. The external cortical system will awaken only very gradually. But if the child is led to find himself in a rather unsatisfactory situation, there will be a prematuration of the system; his senses will awaken precociously and the child will use understanding as a defence system against traumatism. Normally, the mind or intelligence is good: thanks to its possibilities of memorizing part experiences, the mind will allow continuity to be re-established, for example, when there has been discontinuity, by virtue of the fact that the child, after a state of excitation, with an attitude that is both erotic and aggressive, passes to a position of dependence in order to receive cares. However the mind, that is to say, intellectual activity, may be a bad thing that leads at first to a false system, in the wrong direction, without belonging to the body. A certain type of mental functioning – such as memorizing or cataloguing impingements with a view to assimilation at later stages of development – may be a burden for the psyche-soma, or for the continuity of existence that constitutes the self. This type of mental functioning acts as a foreign body if it is associated with inadequate adaptation to the environment.

TRUE SELF, FALSE SELF

If the true self derives from the life of bodily tissue and from the free play of bodily functions, including that of the heart and breathing, it does hardly more than bring together the details of experience bound up with the fact of living.

60

Winnicott stresses that the idea of the false self, as far as he can see, may be found in Freud's earliest formulations and he draws a parallel with the distinction made by Freud between a central part governed by the drives (or by what Freud calls sexuality, pre-genital or genital) and a part turned outwards, establishing relations with the world.[13]

When a false self is organized in an individual who has a very high intellectual potential, the mind will tend to become the locus in which the false self resides. There is a dissociation between intellectual activity and psychosomatic existence.[14] If there is this double anomaly:

(a) The organization of a false self in order to conceal the true self.
(b) An attempt on the part of the individual to resolve his problem by using a brilliant intellect.

The clinical table that results may very easily take others in. A normal equivalent of the false self appears in any individual in a healthy state, for in the true self there is a certain quality of obedience that corresponds to the infant's capacity to subject himself and not to expose himself. The capacity for compromise is an acquisition.[15]

In the extreme examples of false self, subjection and imitation are in the forefront. There is almost a personal line through imitation: the child succeeds in playing a role, that of the true self as it would have been if it had existed.

On the patient of *Holding and Interpretation*, Winnicott relates:

'He came to analysis saying that he could not talk freely, he had no small talk or imaginative or play capacity, and that he could not make a spontaneous gesture or get excited. . . . Gradually it became clear that he was listening to conversations that were going on within, and reporting any parts of these conversations that he thought might interest me. In time, it could be said that he brought himself to analysis and talked about himself, as a mother or father might bring a child to me and talk about him. In these early phases (lasting six months) I had no chance of direct conversation with the child (himself).'[16]

61

To return to development, it is logical, concludes Winnicott, to contrast psyche and soma and consequently the emotional development and the somatic development of an individual. But the mental and physical are not of the same kind. 'Mental phenomena are complications of variable importance in the continuity of the existence of the psyche-soma, in what accumulates to form the self of the individual.'

## The self and the incommunicable inner life

Thus the mental health of the individual is built up on the mother's care, which is hardly noticeable when everything goes well and is the continuation of the physiological contribution characteristic of the pre-natal period. The life of the tissues and the good working of the various functions that, for the infant, provide the ego with a silent, but vital support, also continue to be provided by the environment. Similarly, schizophrenia or infantile psychosis, or a predisposition to later psychoses, are bound up with the failure in the environment. This does not mean however that the harmful effects of this failure cannot be described in terms of ego distortions and defences against primitive anxieties, that is to say, in terms of the individual. The work of Melanie Klein on the defence mechanisms by splitting and on projection and introjection, etc., represents an attempt to define, in terms of the individual the effects of the failure of the environment. This work on the primitive mechanism explains only part of the history, Winnicott goes on; for the other part we must turn to a reconstitution of the environment and its failures.

The source of the infant's gesture expressing a spontaneous impulse is the true self and the gesture indicates the existence of a potential true self. Winnicott links there the idea of a true self with the spontaneous gesture; at this period in the individual's development, the fusion of motility and of erotic elements takes place, then the infant begins to play with the illusion of creation and of omnipotent control. Later, he becomes capable of recognizing the illusory element, the fact of playing and imagining. This is the basis of the symbol, which at first is both spontaneity or hallucination on the part of the child and also an external object created and, ultimately, cathected.

1st February 1968.

# 5  Winnicott the clown[1]

'We'll send you a knife to cut your dreams up, and we'll send our fingers to lift things up, and we'll send some balls of snow to lick when the snow comes and we'll send you some crayons to draw a man with. We'll send you a suit to wear when you go to college.

'With best wishes to your flowers and your trees and your fish in your fishpool.

Love from,<br>Gabrielle

'We are coming to see you with best wishes in our heads.'[2]

This letter, one might almost call it poem, from his young patient introduces us to a world of fantasy. Winnicott's love of play and his 'moral courage'[3] are revealed throughout his work. Does he not confront danger head on with, for example, the children he helped, elucidating their anti-social tendency, to rediscover, in their environment, their continuity of life with the adolescents, stuck in the doldrums, with the borderline cases?

His physical presence, his ease, his grace, his squiggle games, in which his dazzling intuition was combined with a technique rooted in theory and experience – everything about him was reminiscent of the circus clown, defying balance without appearing to do so.

## Winnicott, the man and his language

'The treatment of an already exciting work with a splash of paint' (as he writes of his use of the word fantasy)[4] raises questions about Winnicott's style, language, his 'philosophical platform'.

Thus he does not hesitate to contrast – and this is no accident! – the use of 'self' and that of 'counter-transference'.[5] 'We can use words as we like, especially artificial words like counter-transference. A word like "self" naturally knows more than we do; it uses us, and can command us.'

In that article on the counter-transference, he refers to 'professional attitude', a special state in which the analyst finds himself when he is working and notes that a reaction is not a counter-transference. However there is a great deal to be said about the use that the analyst may make of his conscious and unconscious reactions to the impact produced in particular by certain patients on his – the analyst's – personality and its repercussions on his professional attitude. This would leave us free to study what Margaret Little calls 'the analyst's total response to the patient's needs' in these cases, while leaving the term counter-transference its own meaning of 'that which we hope to eliminate by selection and analysis and the training of analysts'.

Donald Woods Winnicott, 'a Protestant by birth', says Masud Khan, 'a nonconformist', came from an artistic family. This businessman's son was brought up in a typically provincial English setting in which everybody was musical and one of his sisters became a talented painter. Winnicott himself played the piano and sang with a tenor voice.

Throughout his life he found his friends among artists, musicians, dancers, painters, sculptors (in the British Institute of Psycho-Analysis there is a bust of him by one of his friends). He was the inspiration behind the committee set up to erect a statue of Freud, by Oscar Nemon in Swiss Cottage. His secretary, Joyce Coles, told me (Jeannine Kalmanovitch) that Winnicott was delighted at the thought that the children would clamber up on to the great man's head while playing. The Piggle is not far away!

But, above all, he wrote; he wrote up his cases, he wrote

poems, but he also drew.[6] This reminds us of the squiggles, which deserve a chapter to themselves.

Style and concepts went together, his ideas were locked together, one inside another; if, according to Winnicott, reparation takes the form of cushions and a blanket, he himself says about regression: 'I think it is not useful to use the word regression whenever infantile behaviour appears in a case history. . . . When we speak of regression in psychoanalysis we imply the existence of an ego organization and a threat of chaos.'[7]

What are we to make of his remark: 'What you will get out of me you will have to extract from chaos?' Chaos, 'between heaven and earth', is not far away from Winnicott's area of symbolic and paradoxical play between fantasy and reality. Thanks to his creative style, Winnicott provided only part of the organization of his ideas: the rest he left to his reader to create.

He sees creativity as 'a colouring of the whole attitude to external reality'.[8]

Paradox runs throughout his concepts and formulations: playing, impingement and defence, true and false self, 'illusion' in relation to 'disillusion'; 'personalization' in relation to 'depersonalization'; integration, non-integration, disintegration; deprivation and hope in the anti-social tendency, presence/absence, the capacity to be alone in the presence of another, fear of breakdown . . .

Starting out from the light he throws on infants during the period of 'hesitation'[9] – a keyword that evokes mental conflict with its bodily participation – he was to say about the psychoanalysis of adults: 'Each interpretation is the glittering object which excites the patient's greed.' One can think of many other formulations that have become familiar since. They also varied according to his audience, for many of his writings were originally spoken.

Winnicott always remained extremely present in the most varied environments; he had obviously kept contact with his first field of action and took great pleasure in addressing not only paediatricians, but also teachers, priests, and doctors. Then there were his talks on the radio. His language could be simple and clear, to the surprise of himself and others; he knew how to adapt it to his audience, often using 'laughter like a banana skin'.[10]

## The body and shared reality

As a doctor, a paediatrician, and a psychoanalyst, Winnicott gave the body its due place: whether he accompanied this child and his mother to the ear, nose, and throat specialist, held this patient's head, or refrained from doing so.[11] Then there was the case of the boy whom the Winnicotts took into their home for three months. After frequently running away – as he had regularly done throughout his life from various institutions – he directed his aggression inside the home, making the Winnicotts' life hell. After each maniacal attack Winnicott threw the boy out, not omitting to tell him that he hated him. (When he had calmed down, the boy could be readmitted by ringing a special bell.)[12]

Masud Khan,[13] who describes 'the balance of his bodily presence', writes: 'In him the psyche and the soma were in constant dialogue.' For Winnicott, 'creativity is inherent in the fact of living . . . and allows the individual (if he is not sick) an approach to external reality.'[14] Whatever happens to someone is creative unless it is undermined by the environment.

Marion Milner wondered 'what exactly he meant by that'. Sometimes he seems to be talking about a particular way of looking at the world, sometimes about a way of doing something deliberately,[15] and sometimes quite simply to be taking pleasure in a bodily activity, for example, taking pleasure in breathing.

'She (Piggle) took the two curtains in the middle of the room and rushed backwards and forwards with them . . .
  '*Gabrielle*: "I am the wind; look out!"'
  'I referred to breathing, the essential element in being alive, something which could not be enjoyed before birth.'[16]

We have seen how he links breath and illusion[17] when he stresses children's interest in bubbles and clouds, rainbows, and other mysterious phenomena. Is it not impossible to decide whether the breath comes originally from the inside or the out?

On the subject of the patient who taught him so much about regression (he takes up her case again in several of his articles), he describes 'a temporary phase in which the breathing of the body was everything'.

> 'I maintained a continuity by my own breathing while she let herself go, abandoned herself, knew nothing. What made my role effective was that I could see her chest and hear her breathing (like a bird), which allowed me to know that she was alive.
>
> 'It was then, that for the first time, she was capable of having a psyche, a personal entity, a body that breathed and moreover, the beginning of a fantasy belonging to the breathing and to the other physiological functions.'[18]

For

> 'it is only from non-existence that existence can begin. . . . The individual cannot develop from the root of the ego if that root is separated from psychosomatic experience and from primary narcissism. It is precisely there that the intellectualization of the ego functions begins. . . . All this is situated temporarily well before what one might rightly call the self is constructed.'[19]

> 'Feeling real is more than existing; it is finding a way to exist as oneself, and to relate to objects as oneself, and to have a self into which to retreat for relaxation.'[20]

Winnicott relates how he often relaxed while writing interpretations that he refrained from making (the case of the patient whom he saw for two-and-a-half or three hours without making a sound for long intervals; the case of boredom in *Holding and Interpretation*).

Later, when he knew that he was seriously ill with heart disease, he had, says André Green, a whole life technique in order never to lose sight of the fact that he had something inside him still left to live.

It is on the subject of a quest for the self[21] that he speaks of 'a new experience . . . one of a non-purposive state, as one might say a sort of ticking over of the unintegrated personality'.[22] Referring to the essential facts that encourage relaxation, he writes:

'In terms of free association this means that the patient on the couch or the child patient among the toys on the floor must be allowed to communicate a succession of ideas, thoughts, impulses, sensations that are not linked except in some way that is neurological or physiological and perhaps beyond detection. That is to say: it is where there is purpose or where there is anxiety or where there is lack of trust based on the need for defence that the analyst will be able to recognize and to point out the connection (or several connections) between the various components of free association material.'[23]

During the third session of a relaxation group[24] the organizer made a particularly long introduction, describing the arms; this introduction was perceived by the observer not so much in her words as in her rhythm and the organizer invited a repetition in three stages: 'then came the moment to start again. . . . Everybody can do as he likes . . . following his own rhythm.'

A long silence.

Then came a few interventions from participants, with references to the empty and the full, words and silence. Here are a few of them:

*Jean-Paul*: 'Above all I felt my body . . . rocked . . . like a disturbing element. There . . . it was soothing, it floated; I had the physical impression of a raft . . . it was pleasanter.'

*Viviane*: '. . . very preoccupied because I was aware from time to time that I was no longer breathing. The breathing no longer soothed me, but took on a very broad, very slow rhythm. It was very relaxing. I felt . . . I was . . . lacking oxygen. It didn't soothe me. . . . not like in childbirth.'

*Pierre*: 'I was separated from my physical principle, that is to say, both relaxed and incapable of escaping the rhythm of life.'

Thus, spontaneously, for some, breathing became the vector of a felt complex in which anxiety and pleasure both played a part. Did this produce an echo in the group of something unexpressed in the introduction?

The observer noted that one of the organizers had trouble with her arms, got breathless while touching participants after the introduction and felt a need of air and solitude, while the other was extremely anxious, was prevented by a cold from making the introduction or taking part in it![24]

On the practice of relaxation, Winnicott, reminding us that 'one of the aims of psychosomatic illness is to draw the psyche from the mind back to the original intimate association with the soma' (hence the 'positive value of the somatic disturbance in its work of counteracting a "seduction" of the psyche into the mind'), notes that methods of relaxation, at their best, enable the future mother to become body-conscious and (if she is not a mental case) such methods help her to a continuity of being and enable her to live as a psyche-soma.[25]

Marion Milner [26] declares that there is a link between the simple pleasure taken in breathing, mentioned by Winnicott, and a whole collection of observations 'obtained through intro-spection both in the clinical situation and in experiments in concentration'.[27]

She makes a connection with the effects produced, on the perception of the object, by the change that occurs in awareness of our own body, and with the opposite set of phenomena, namely,

> 'the effects of certain kinds of concentrating on the object . . . on one's own body awareness . . . the change in body aware-ness, a change to a sense of wholeness, the totality of all the proprioceptive sensations; in fact, not a body-image, but a body-perception . . . concerned with the actual coenaesthesic awareness of its existence in space and time, including espec-ially the sense of one's own weight and the feelings of one's own breathing. . . . I have also noticed that when it did happen there was . . . not the narcissistic impoverishment of one's relation to the external world . . . but an actual enrich-ment of it . . . a sense of well-being that is of a different kind from that which results from lack of tension between the ego and the superego when feeling one has lived up to one's standards.'

A parallel is drawn with the presentation of the body that does not have precise limits and of the child's earliest not-me possession or transitional object, often a soft object, which may partly suggest the 'fuzziness of the sense of the body boundary in direct sensation'.

'I suspected too,' Marion Milner adds, 'that Winnicott himself knew a lot about this kind of relation to the body and that it could have played a large part in those child-therapeutic consultations where he used what he called the squiggle game.'

J.-B. Pontalis says,

'The squiggle game is a technique of communication discovered by its inventor in his paediatric consultations and in
child psychiatry. Dr Winnicott makes a squiggle in front of the
child; the child turns it into . . . and so on, either Winnicott
proposing another squiggle, or the child making one, which
Winnicott changes in turn: on the basis of the few lines drawn
on a sheet of paper, to which each gives a shape, meaning
begins to circulate. In my opinion, this is a very different
method from a "projection test", even if the author has made
such a comparison. Indeed, in this exchange, in this inventive, shared game, is constituted what might be called a
"transitional space", by analogy with what the author calls
transitional phenomena. The method gives rise to a
process.'[28]

Winnicott stresses that

'what happens in the game and in the whole interview
depends on the use made of the child's experience, including
the material that presents itself.

In order to use the mutual experience one must have in one's
bones a theory of the emotional development of the child and of
the relationship of the child to the environmental factors.'[29]

'The humour and acuity of the line,' to use J.-B. Pontalis's
words, are to be found in one's personal squiggles, which are
sometimes frightening, sometimes highly amusing. We have
seen a collection of them exhibited at the International Congress
in London. Clare Winnicott tells how a new one awaited her
every morning at breakfast and that, if they were separated, she
received one by post each day. Were they not, then, subjective
objects thus projected into the field of shared reality as well as an
aspect of creative motility? One might cite in this regard Anne
Clancier's work on the creation of poets in absence and
separation.[30]

What takes place between the subject and the object when
there is no potential space? Thus tearing one's hair is a negative

*Winnicott and Paradox*

way of denying separation, although it is not the only one: there is neither the room nor the depression necessary for creation, as described by Renata Gaddini in relation to the objects that serve as *precursors* to the transitional object – a notion that attracted Winnicott's attention. He was delighted that such work was being done and felt a sense of relief at 'passing on the torch'.

'The potential space between baby and mother, between child and family, between individual and society or the world, depends on experience which leads to trust. It can be looked upon as sacred to the individual in that it is here that the individual experiences creative living.'[31]

To return to 'Winnicott in person' and to his own spaces we have imagined, with Clare Winnicott, Donald as a child, running, cycling, playing rugby, singing in the choir. Reading aloud, preferably sitting on the floor, has remained a traditional way of spending evenings at home. We have seen him in Paddington, during his consultations, jumping over rows of chairs to join children, or in the confines of a working space. We have only to read 'The Observation of Infants in a Set Situation', in which the place of each individual is defined: the mother and the child, the spatula on the table, etc. We should note his descriptions: seats adopted by one or other of his patients or by himself – high, low, sofas, their colour, during sometimes very long sessions; the role of the curtain, which separates or brings together, the space of the office and that of the play corner, without forgetting the wider environment – the view of the flowers in the window-boxes or on the roof garden, the doors, the waiting-room, etc., as well as what is in that space: blankets, cushions, the glass of water, the kettle, depending on the case.

In the case of the Piggle we see him rolling the ruler[32] or playing the role of the hungry baby, striking himself and getting angry. His secretary, Joyce Coles, recounts that he left his sessions with little Gabrielle red-faced, dishevelled, and breathless (he was already very sick at the time, about 1964) and went and dictated his notes straight away.

Marion Milner evokes trapeze artists observed one day on a village square to describe the motility displayed by Winnicott before he could start work:

'Down below was a little clown, in a grey floppy coat too big for him, fooling around while the others did their stuff, occasionally making a fruitless attempt to jump up and reach the bar. Then, all of a sudden, he made a huge leap and there he was, whirling around on the bar, all his clothes flying out, like a huge Catherine Wheel, and with roars of delight from the crowd. I knew this was my image of Winnicott, because often, over the years when we had a gap of time and we had arranged to meet and discuss some theoretical problem, he would open the door and then be all over the place, whistling, forgetting something, running upstairs, a general sort of clatter, so that I would be impatient for him to settle down. But, gradually, I came to see this as a necessary preliminary for the fiery flashes of intuition that would follow, when he did finally settle down. I even found the logic of it described in one of his papers, where he talks of the necessity, while doing an analysis, to recognize and to allow for phases of nonsense, when no thread must be looked for in the patient's material, because what is going on is the preliminary chaos that is the first phase of the creative process.'[33]

What was this little clown like?

In 1952, D. W. Winnicott had been asked to interview students as a result of latent problems within the Société psychanalytique de Paris. Dr E. Martin relates how,

'As luck would have it, I was interviewed by him and found myself in front of a quite extraordinary individual. I can't quite remember his height, he struck me as being of average height or on the small side. He looked like a stage Englishman – he was wearing a sort of large, very long Raglan overcoat. I don't exactly remember the colour of his eyes, but they were extremely intelligent. Right from the start he gave a sense of empathy, seeming to imply "whatever you have to say about the Lacan affair I know already, but I'd be delighted to hear what you have to say about it". Later, I was interviewed by Mme L. and I was able to see that these were not my own projections. Mme L. appeared like a normal person, in the usual sense of the term, whereas Winnicott, at least for me with my type of personality, was quite extraordinary.'[34]

73

Anne Clancier has recounted her personal impressions in a seminar given at the Institut E. Claparède:

'I was one of those whom he questioned when he came with that celebrated commission of enquiry. . . . At first I was rather intimidated by such an important individual, but, with Winnicott, one felt immediately at ease. . . . What struck me most about that little man was his eyes, which, although they looked shut, nevertheless shone brightly. He questioned us, but they were not at all the same questions as those posed by Mme L. – they were rather odd questions and one didn't know what he was getting at. At the same time, one felt a kind of empathy – it was really very strange.'

It is striking that his height should have aroused so many reactions – 'But he was so small!' Or 'he seemed small' – whether one had known him or seen him at a seminar, or on a conference platform, or had attended one of his consultations. Seeing him playing on the floor with his young patients or imagining him with the Piggle might suggest the picture of a grandfather with his grandchildren. It is as if people recreated Winnicott with the size of the child that is in us, the size that a child at ease with this gentleman, this old gentleman, one might say, might give him. It must have been the same kind of communication without a shared language that he had with the children of a Danish psychoanalyst, delighted at seeing him again. 'At last an Englishman we can talk to,' they said, and were then astonished to be reminded that he did not speak Danish. A tall young woman who danced with Winnicott (he loved dancing) during a conference noted that she felt definitely small. Leni Iselin's dramatic photograph, taken shortly before his death, recreates that impression; the private photographs of 1962,[35] show him on the roof garden referred to in *The Piggle* surrounded by flowers, still quite tall, even if he was no longer the athlete of his student years.

Anybody who talks about Winnicott refers to his presence. Masud Khan remembers

'the extraordinary tranquillity emanating from that somatic presence, at once balanced and sparkling, that he possessed when he was sitting and "holding" the regressed patient in the clinical situation. Only those of us who have had the privilege to be his patients and were the *object of his care* can testify to his unique quality of attention, psychical as well as somatic.'[36]

He himself refers in his works to this concentration, through his capacity to maintain a completely still attentiveness. It is as if one let the patient drop, he says, reproducing one of his primitive agonies when one is not giving the patient one's entire attention at the right moment – which did not prevent him, of course, from noting in *The Piggle* his moments of somnolence, relating them to the case itself as much as to his own tiredness.[37] Elsewhere he notes: 'When a patient is engaged in discovering the aggressive root the analyst is more exhausted by the process, one way or another, than when the patient is discovering the erotic root of the instinctual life.' He is referring to individuals in whom 'it is very common to find large quantities of unfused aggression' that, in analysis, must be confronted separately, since the patient 'in the transference cannot achieve a fusion of the two'.[38]

He could also laugh heartily with his young patients. His face, Gillespie tells us,[39] was as lined at thirty-five as at seventy and bore the marks of his ceaseless intellectual quest, constantly scrutinizing his own approach.

One of his patients asked him for an enlargement of his photograph in order to examine the lines on 'that old landscape'.[40] 'I sent her the photograph . . . she needed to hear that my lined face was marked in a way that bore no relation to the rigidity of her mother's and nanny's faces.'

This bodily presence, his face, his eyes, gave him a peculiar radiance. This is illustrated by an incident recounted by the French psychoanalyst Eva Rosenblum: some years earlier, on the occasion of a conference, she was standing on the platform of a London station. The atmosphere was grey and misty. Suddenly she saw Winnicott on the platform. She knew him only through attending a pre-congress seminar and had also met him, glass in hand, at a party. Her own reaction surprised her a great deal. She went up to him and said: 'Oh! When I see you the sun comes out,' or something of the sort. 'I could never remember,' she said, 'whether I felt shy at going up to a gentleman I knew so little and saying something like that!'

How did he become this Winnicott?

## Winnicott: his training and personal ideas

He was a doctor and a philosopher, and talked brilliantly if he felt in sympathy. There was no aspect of life, morality, art, or politics that he did not throw fresh light on, revealing some hitherto unperceived truth, just as an artist shows us some familiar object in some unexpected light, giving it new meaning.[41]

TRAINING

Without losing any of his charm, he became with the years a 'consummate master of psychoanalysis and no doubt of self-analysis'.[42] He describes his intellectual odyssey as being rooted in 'the very great developments that took place in London in the twenty years after the end of World War I'.[43]

'From my point of view,' Winnicott adds, 'psychoanalysis in England was an edifice whose foundation was Ernest Jones . . . to whom I went when I found I needed help in 1923.' He put him in touch with James Strachey, to whom he went for analysis for ten years.

Stressing the interaction of his analysis, his research, and his clinical work,[44] he recounts how hard he tried to get 'innumerable mothers to describe their infants' way of life in the early stages before the mother has got out of touch with these intimate things'. His tireless scientific interest was revealed when he wrote that, if it were given to him to begin all over again, he would devote his life to observing infancy. If his own analysis took him towards the forgotten territory of his own childhood, the analysis of children gave him, he says, a child's view of infancy. His psychoanalytic training and his basic training cases took him to early infantile mental mechanisms as displayed in dreams and symptoms.

The care brought to case-histories by Winnicott, who was also trying to apply what he was discovering in his own analysis to the children he saw as a paediatrician, came to Strachey's knowledge, during the analysis. Strachey then advised him to go and see Melanie Klein and said: 'She is saying some things that may or may not be true and you must find out for yourself, for you will not get what Melanie Klein teaches in my analysis of you.'

It was difficult for him, because overnight he had 'changed from being a pioneer into being a student with a pioneer teacher'.[45]

Winnicott's second analyst was Joan Riviere, who was close to Melanie Klein.[46] A new stage began:

'Then I came to the analysis of patients who proved to be borderline, or who came to have the mad part of them met and altered. It is work with borderline patients that has taken me (whether I have liked it or not)[47] to the early human condition, and here I mean to the early life of the individual rather than to the mental mechanisms of earliest infancy.'

To do this, Winnicott employs the professional attitude,

'which is rather like symbolism, in that it assumes a *distance between analyst and patient*, [for] the symbol is in the gap between the subjective object and the object that is perceived objectively. . . . Now I say this without fear because I am not an intellectual and in fact I personally do my work very much from the body-ego, so to speak. But I think of myself in my analytic work working with easy but conscious mental effort.'[48]

RESEARCH

As a researcher and lonely clinician, obstinate and modest, Winnicott always maintained his independence of mind, his originality of thought. In his view independents ought to remain independent, rather than handing themselves over to a leader. Was this one of the reasons why he kept his distance from Melanie Klein?

Dr D. W. Winnicott 87 Chester Square SW1 01-730 9544

7.1.71.

Dear Mr Jeanneret K

Thank you for your letter 2 Jan. Before (and your reply reactions and references I want to know if

CHRISTMAS
1959
NEW YEAR
1960

GREETINGS
to
Joyce & Arthur Coles
from
Drs & Mrs D.W. WINNICOTT.

87 CHESTER SQUARE
LONDON SW1

---

Christmas 1955
New Year 1956
Greetings!
to
Mr & Mrs Coles
from
Dr & Mrs D.W.Winnicott.

I'm s[orr]y my letter. I seem
to have written 3 that I am
not sure you got. Could you
remember to if you got this
and so I wrote 2 or 3 more

so?

yours very gratefully

[signature]

As Chiland notes,[49] Winnicott never constructs an article on a polemical argument or as a theoretical demonstration, but around what he has felt in his relationships with others. Speaking of 'the gap between theory and practice', Chiland asks the following question: would *Holding and Interpretation* have been published without revisions and comments if Winnicott had had the time to make them before he died? She poses certain questions about the man and the work. Does the work belong to the potential area? We never know what an analyst does, but only what he says he does. And in transforming the openness of his thought, which proceeded by associations, around an idea or a word, into a closed system, one is failing to take into account the fact that Winnicott himself said that he allowed himself 'considerable latitude' in following the theme wherever it took him.[50]

Although he was unmoved by the criticisms of his colleagues, while respecting them, he proved very open to his questioners and took great care to avoid hurting their susceptibilities. Profound respect for others was the key to the self-training that he inspired around him, in neighbouring disciplines, from paediatrics and psychoanalysis to education and social work.[51]

Furthermore, appealing to the 'maternal fibre'[52] in everybody, Winnicott remarked that 'the need to discover and to recognize the worth of the ordinary good mother' played an important role as far as he was concerned. Although taking an interest in the mothers was also to take an interest in the fathers, he felt a profound need to address the mothers and explain what he was trying to discover: 'the meaning of the word devotion and the possibility of recognizing in a quite vague, but deeply felt way, what I owe my own mother'.[53] Here a man is in a more difficult situation than a woman. He obviously cannot reward his mother by becoming a mother in turn. He has no other alternative than to go as far as possible towards an awareness of what the mother successfully produced in him.

'One of the solutions, for a man who is fascinated by this problem, is to take part in an objective study of the role of the mother, above all of the role that she plays at the beginning.'

Nevertheless Winnicott insisted on the cruel aspects of maternal love, which is associated with aggressiveness and destructiveness. Indeed, it is necessary, he says, that the parent – or the therapist – should fail the child (the patient), but in small doses for 'the child has need of an external object that is not only an object that brings him satisfaction'.

Thus there appears once again the movement backwards and forwards, the breath of language, which corresponds to the inspiration and expiration of the flux of development in the primitive parent–child interaction. Does not the keyword 'transitional' serve as a bridge between the individual and later cultural symbolic levels?

10th April 1969.

# 6 Creativity: transitional phenomena and transitional objects

If the title of this chapter reverses the usual order and refers to transitional phenomena before transitional objects, it is to draw attention to the development of Winnicott's ideas between the writing of his 1951 article, 'Transitional Objects and Transitional Phenomena' and that of his book *Playing and Reality* of 1971. The author explains his position in the introduction to the latter work. Over those twenty years, Winnicott had come to realize that readers interested in his ideas had given special status to the bit of rag or teddy bear or some other object, whose use he has described in terms of a transitional object, to the detriment of a whole range of broader phenomena. Now he is referring not so much to 'the object used as the use of the object'. This involves a paradox that must be accepted and tolerated and respected, without being resolved.

In order to achieve an understanding of this paradox, without 'flight to split off intellectual functioning', with consequent 'loss of the value of the paradox itself', it is necessary to retrace the history of transitional phenomena and of their precursors in the baby.

Although the intermediate area, the field of experience between the 'me' and the 'not-me', has been referred to by philosophers, poets, and artists, Winnicott was the first clinician and theoretician to have grasped the importance of transitional *phenomena*, beginning with *transitional space*. He set out from the observation of babies, who, from birth, use their hands, their fingers, both to satisfy oral drives and to find peace and quiet. The importance of this erogenous zone and of these auto-erotic activities are followed, a few months later, by activities of a different kind. The babies then privilege an object: a doll, a teddy bear, a bit of sheet or blanket, to which they become attached in a 'habitual and tyrannical' way. This is what Winnicott calls the transitional object.

The notion of a time interval between the two phenomena is really important. Indeed, with the transitional object we are presented with something quite different from oral excitement and satisfaction. It is a relationship with a concrete object that is no longer the child's body. It is, says Winnicott, 'the first *Not-Me* possession'. The child becomes passionately attached to it and often can only sleep when that object is near him. Usually he brings it to his mouth, or strokes his cheek with it; indeed he may at the same time indulge in such auto-erotic activities as thumb sucking. Sometimes the infant's babbling or someone else's humming may play the role of transitional object.

'One may suppose that thinking, or fantasying gets linked up with these functional experiences.' Winnicott calls all such activities transitional phenomena.

These phenomena are 'a defence against anxiety', in particular against anxiety of the depressive type. The appearance of transitional objects is preceded by the use of the *precursor* objects described by Renata Gaddini (1970) and thus named by her with Winnicott's agreement (1968).[1] Winnicott said that the transitional object is paradoxically created by the child whereas the *precursor* objects

'having the capacity of consoling the child in a unique way, are not discovered or invented by the child (R. Gaddini, 1970). They are administered by the mother, or are parts of the child's body, or of the mother's body. The element that precursor objects have in common is that of being introduced into the infant's mouth to integrate the Self, the moment it gets separated from the primary object (the breast). This search for integration has always the "into the mouth model", to respond to the need of filling an emptiness which comes into being with the separation at birth. The "into the mouth P.O." may be associated, in the child, with the search for tactile sensations, such as the mother's hair, or nevi, or ear lobe, or other parts of the body, which later becomes the child's body. What is characteristic of the P.O. is that the fantasies connected are purely reduplicative, and have to do with the body self. The infant who sucks his thumb or his tongue or a pacifier does not reach out from himself. The P.O. is no longer the breast but not yet something separated from the self: it implies the extreme passivity and dependence which belongs to the body language.'

When a transitional object has been picked out by the child, the parents will be able to recognize the value of that object and take it everywhere the child goes. The mother 'lets it get dirty and even smelly, knowing that by washing it she introduces a break in continuity in the infant's experience, a break that may destroy the meaning and value of the object to the infant'.

Transitional phenomena generally appear between the fourth and twelfth month, depending on the baby. These models may survive into a later stage. The object continues to be indispensable at certain moments of solitude, when falling asleep, or when the child is threatened by a sense of depression.

When the child is able to begin using organized sounds, he often gives the transitional object a name; this name is often significant. 'It usually has a word used by the adults partly incorporated in it.' It may, for instance, be the word 'baa', in which the *b* may have come from the adults' use of the word 'baby' or 'bear'.

The account of this naming with the appearance of language, and above all the passage from the expressive function of language to *connative* and *cognitive* functions has been brought out by Michèle Perron-Borelli, in her article 'L'investissement de la signification'.[2] She sets out from an observation of her fourteen-month-old daughter, who, one day, during and because of, it seems, an anxiogenic experience, called for transitional object, a teddy bear, *'gnegne'*. Next day she discovered on the shelf another bear she had never paid attention to before, which she pointed out to her mother, saying in a questioning way: *'gne-gne?'* Thus for the first time this little girl was able to make a semantic generalization. The author shows how the child was able to pass from cathecting the transitional object to cathecting meaning and creativity.

## Particular qualities of the relationship with the transitional object

Winnicott sums up the qualities of this relationship thus:

1. The infant assumes rights over the object and we agree to this assumption.
2. The object is affectionately cuddled as well as excitedly loved and mutilated.
3. It must never change, unless changed by the infant.
4. It must survive instinctual loving, and also hating, and, if it be a feature, pure aggression.
5. Yet it must seem to the infant to give warmth, or to move, or to have texture, or to do something that seems to show it has vitality or reality of its own.
6. It must come from without from our point of view, but not so from the point of view of the baby. Neither does it come from within; it is not an hallucination.
7. Its fate is to be gradually allowed to be decathected, so that in the course of years it becomes not so much forgotten as relegated to limbo.

This last characteristic is important if one wishes to understand the meaning of that object for

'the transitional object does not "go inside" nor does the feeling about it necessarily undergo repression. It is not forgotten and it is not mourned. It loses meaning, and this is because the transitional phenomena have become diffused, have become spread out over the whole intermediate territory between "inner psychic reality" and "the external world as perceived by two persons in common", that is to say, over the whole cultural field.'[3]

The transitional object and phenomena then widen out to embrace the fields of 'play, and of artistic creativity and appreciation, and of religious feeling, and of dreaming, and also of fetishism, lying and stealing, the origin and loss of affectionate feeling, drug addiction, the talisman of obsessional rituals, etc.'[4]

## Relationship of the transitional object to symbolism

Winnicott believes that the transitional object (whatever it is) is symbolic of some part-object such as the breast. Nevertheless,

'the point of it is not its symbolic value so much as its actuality. It's not being the breast (or the mother), although real, is as important as the fact that it stands for the breast (or mother).

'When symbolism is employed the infant is already clearly distinguishing between fantasy and fact, between inner objects and external objects, between primary creativity and perception. But the term transitional object, according to my suggestion, gives room for the process of becoming able to accept difference and similarity. I think there is use for a term for the root of symbolism in time, a term that describes the infant's journey from the purely subjective to objectivity; and it seems to me that the transitional object (piece of blanket, etc.) is what we see of this journey of progress towards experiencing.'

One cannot understand what this object is without understanding fully the nature of symbolism. 'It seems that symbolism can be properly studied only in the process of the growth of an individual and that it has at the very best a variable meaning.'[5]

## Theoretical study

Setting out from analytical theory, Winnicott observes:

1. The transitional object stands for the breast, or the object of the first relationship.
2. The transitional object antedates established reality-testing.

3. In relation to the transitional object the infant passes from (magical) omnipotent control to control by manipulation (involving muscle eroticism and co-ordination pleasure).
4. The transitional object may eventually develop into a fetish object and so persist as a characteristic of the adult sexual life.
5. The transitional object may, because of anal erotic organization, stand for faeces (but it is not for this reason that it may become smelly and remain unwashed).[6]

Comparing the concept of the transitional object with Melanie Klein's concept of the internal object Winnicott writes: 'The transitional object is *not an internal object* (which is a mental concept) – it is a possession. Yet it is not (for the infant) an external object either.'

## The pathology of the transitional object

Sometimes certain children use an object to deny separation with the mother.

Winnicott illustrates this denial with a clinical case, that of the boy with the string:

A boy aged seven was brought to Winnicott's consultation by his father and mother. The parents also brought with them their two daughters, aged ten and four. The boy presented a series of symptoms of a characteral order as well as some compulsions. The parents forgot to mention an important detail that Winnicott discovered later. He started to draw a squiggle and was struck by the fact that in this game all the drawings were associated with string: a lassoo, a whip, the string of a yo-yo, a knot, etc. When Winnicott saw the parents again, he asked them why the child was so continually interested in string. They had forgotten to mention it; they then told how their son was obsessed by string and that whenever he went into a room in the house, they were liable to find that he had tied together chairs and tables, or they might find that a cushion, for instance, was tied to the fireplace. Recently, which had worried the parents a great deal, the boy had tied a string around his sister's neck (the sister whose birth caused the first separation of this boy from his mother). The following year the mother had had a depression that forced her to spend two months in a psychiatric hospital, thus causing a new separation with the boy. Winnicott explained to the mother that her son feared separation and was trying to deny it by playing with string. He asked her to explain this to her son, at the right moment.

Six months later, the parents came back and the mother said that after having interpreted the string game to her son, he had immediately stopped it; later, the game had begun again; the mother had then had to go into hospital for an operation; she had again interpreted the fear of separation to her son and reassured him. After this conversation, the game stopped once more.

Four years later, he began playing with the string again as a result of a new depression, on the part of the mother. The boy had then played at hanging himself by the feet and had simulated death, which had brought about the hasty arrival of the mother, who was very moved when she saw him. Then the boy became very affectionate with his mother, concerned himself a great deal with her, and gave her toys, which he regarded as his children. It seemed that he had then made a maternal identification 'based on his own insecurity in relation to his mother, and that this could develop into homosexuality. In the same way the preoccupation with string could develop into a perversion.'[7]

In a note, added years later, Winnicott admitted that he had come to see that this boy could not be cured of his illness. The tie-up with the mother's depressive illness remained, and it was impracticable to give him psychotherapy at home.

'In adolescence this boy developed new addictions, especially to drugs, and he could not leave home in order to receive education. All attempts to get him placed away from his mother failed because he regularly escaped and ran back home.'

Winnicott wonders if a specialist in drug addiction, making a study of this case, would pay proper respect to 'the psychopathology manifested in the area of transitional phenomena'.

This case may be compared with trichotillomania (a compulsion to pull hair), which may be understood as an attempt to rediscover part of the mother's body, but also as a denial of separation. Renata Gaddini, however, sees this symptom as a pathological model more of the precursor object than of the transitional object. She believes that these observations are able to throw light on the pathology of identity. Winnicott, who found them extremely interesting, remarked: 'What I want to say is that I value very much the work that you are doing. It is especially true that I have not had time, or perhaps inclination, to develop the relationship between transitional objects and pacifiers (dummies). The patterns that you describe fascinate me' (letter of 5 September 1968 to Renata Gaddini).

Thus we see that, right up to the last, Winnicott was trying to deepen his understanding of the transitional phenomena and took an interest in any research being made in this field.

Renata Gaddini also includes merycism (or rumination), described by Michel Soulé,[8] in the pathology of the precursor object. In his case

'the food or milk is repeatedly brought back into the mouth, and the mouth is full of milk, and then in part it flows at his mouth corners and in part is again swallowed. It is typically the tongue which initiates the process of rumination, in function of the lost nipple (or thumb, or pacifier). But this time the child can recreate the experience of self-feeding indefinitely, reproducing for himself those sensations which were connected with his mother's feeding him. With his imitative fantasy, he masters self-loss and controls his fear of returning to a non-integrated state.'[9]

There is a great difference between the imitative fantasy of these ruminating children and the maturing illusion of the normal three-month-old infant who creates the breast for himself. The illusion of omnipotence gives the child the idea that he has created the breast himself. Soon frustrations come and he has to learn that omnipotence does not last forever. But his illusion has been the fundamental element of his maturational process; and it stems from this that the development of mentalization is highly stimulated. This brings us to stress once again the maturing value of the transitional phenomena, unlike the phenomena bound up with the precursor object.

In the transitional area primitive creative activity is already at work. It is the emergence from auto-eroticism, but there may also be a persistence of the latter in the form of a pleasure in functioning.

On the basis of this primitive illusion, the subject experiences satisfaction in manipulating objects, but if the satisfaction is sufficient in itself, there is no exchange between the mother and the child and such an exchange cannot be structured.[10]

One may wonder whether there may not have been, in cases of alcoholism and various addictions even more than in psychoses, an inadequacy of symbolization.

## Dreaming, fantasying, living

These cases may be compared with the adult patients described by Winnicott in terms of *fantasying*.[11] In this pathological fantasy activity, which, according to him, is very different from dreaming, it is as if the psychical apparatus functions without a load in an almost constant fantasy activity in which one can see no elaboration. Thus the subject would remain in the area of illusion and make no distinction between illusion and reality, which is not the case with creative daydreaming or with dreaming when the subject remembers his dream. This might be interpreted as a result of splitting. In fantasying, the fantasy activity assumes the value of a fetish object.

Fantasying may be compared with the rumination of obsessional neurotics. It might be described as a neurotic activity, though Winnicott does not use the term, for it is 'an isolated phenomenon, absorbing energy but not contributing in either to dreaming or to living'. He shows this very clearly through a clinical case of a woman who herself draws a distinction between these two modes of activity. For him fantasying seemed to be a flight into the imaginary, impoverishing because it absorbed energy, whereas dreaming was a mode of imagination that enriched life. In this case dreaming, which was actually living, was to be in relationship with real objects. This patient showed clearly that dreaming and living belonged to one set of phenomena whereas for her daydreaming was a sterile fantasy activity of a different order.

Winnicott also recounts the case of an adult patient for whom he realized that only absence was real. One day she said to him that for her the negative was more real than the positive, the absence of an object more real than its presence. From the point of view of the long, traumatizing separations suffered by this patient in childhood, Winnicott realized that he had already had, when she had been separated from her parents, transitional objects that were

'symbolical of something and were real for the child; but gradually, or perhaps frequently for a little while, she had to doubt the reality of the things that they were symbolizing. That is to say, if they were symbolical of her mother's devotion and reliability they remained real in themselves but what they stood for was not real. The mother's devotion and reliability were unreal.'

For Winnicott, 'this clinical fragment illustrates the value of keeping in mind the distinctions that exist between phenomena in terms of their position in the area between external or shared reality and the true dream'.

Harold Searles, who has devoted almost all his activity to treating psychotic patients, attaches great importance to transitional phenomena, which he compares with 'therapeutic symbiosis'. He writes,

'I believe that the psychoanalyst and psychotherapist would understand transitional objects and phenomena better if they regarded them as tributaries of a broader domain, that of therapeutic symbiosis, of which they form different facets. In discovering that the symbiotic relationship is constantly threatened, one realizes with less surprise, as have many authors since Winnicott, that this or that particular element in the non-human environment is also experienced by the patient as a "transitional object" – that is to say, existing in the transitional domain between a reality that is not entirely internal and a reality that is not yet entirely external.'[12]

## Playing

For Winnicott, playing is a fundamental activity. Freud confronted this problem in his article on literary creation and daydreaming, when he wrote: 'the poet is like the child playing'. Although Melanie Klein took a great interest in play, it was above all in so far as it concerned its use in child psychotherapy.

Winnicott pays homage to Marion Milner, who, in her work, has made an important contribution to the study of the formation of the symbol and established the relationship between children's play and concentration in the adult.

Marion Milner, an artist as well as a psychoanalyst, has made a particular study of creation in the painter. She writes,

> 'Most of us have probably forgotten the moments when the original poet who is inside us creates, for himself, the external world, discovering the familiar in the nonfamiliar; or we keep them in some secret place in our memories because they are much too like the visitation of the gods to be mixed up with ordinary thought.'[13]

D. W. Winnicott believes that his approach is fairly close to this proposition; however he makes his own analysis of playing.

For him, playing took on new meaning when he studied transitional phenomena and he considered that the study of play had not yet found its place in the psychoanalytical literature.

It was to belong to Winnicott to give it that place. 'Playing has a place and a time.' Play, as a transitional object, is neither inside nor outside. 'To control what is outside one has to *do* things, not simply to think or to wish, and *doing things takes time*. Playing is doing.'

Winnicott's conception is fairly close to the etymology of the word poet (from the Greek *poien* – to make). The poet, the creator, is the individual who makes, who makes something in time, but it is a particular type of activity.


## Paradox

Winnicott stresses the paradox implied in the use of the transitional object. The existence of an intermediate area, neither inside the individual nor outside him, in which cultural experience will gradually become organized, is therefore based on a paradox. For, according to Winnicott, the paradox must be accepted, tolerated, and not be resolved:

'by flight to split-off intellectual functioning, it is possible to resolve the paradox, but the price of this is the loss of the value of the paradox itself. This paradox, once accepted and tolerated, has value for every human individual who is not only alive and living in this world but who is also capable of being infinitely enriched by exploitation of the cultural link with the past and with the future.'

Winnicott remarks that the existence of what may be taken to be an intermediate area has not escaped the attention of philosophers, theologians, or the seventeenth-century metaphysical poets, but that his conception sprang from his study of babies and children.

It is in that transitional area that such cultural phenomena as art and religion are situated.

# Conclusions

## Winnicott's paradoxes

There are many fruitful instances of paradox throughout Winnicott's work. They invariably attest to the originality of his thinking. This is the moment to consider the title of our book: *Winnicott and Paradox*.

Paradox was introduced into psychology by the Palo Alto group. It was then taken up by such researchers as R. D. Laing and introduced into France in the psychoanalytic work of P. C. Racamier (1973),[1] who demonstrated the paradoxality of the thinking of schizophrenics, and by Didier Anzieu (1975),[2] to whom we owe the terms 'paradoxical resistance' and 'paradoxical transference'.

For most authors, paradoxality and the paradoxical transference are processes that are defensive in intention and lead the subject to an impasse. They are either a way of unbinding the death drive (Anzieu), or an anti-conflictual formation that forbids ambivalence and blocks the structuring of the Oedipus complex (Racamier). For Winnicott, on the other hand, paradox is involved in the process of maturation. He introduced the notion of it, without yet using the term, in his article, 'Transitional Objects and Transitional Phenomena' (1951) and he used the word paradox in 'The Capacity To Be Alone' (1958).

Such authors as Jean-Bertrand Pontalis and André Green

have used models proposed by Winnicott in their own work. The first systematic analysis of the Winnicottian paradoxes and of the place of paradox in Winnicott's thought is to be found in the work of René Roussillon.[3]

We have commented on the paradoxes in the course of our book; we shall now list a few of the more fundamental ones to be found in Winnicott's thought.

'Paradox is implied in Winnicott's work in two different ways. First, in the form of logical paradoxes, described as such, which must be accepted if the child is to develop properly; they are essential elements for the establishment of a transitional space necessary to the child's *continuity of being*. Secondly, there are the paradoxical defences, which were not formulated as such by the author and which occur when *continuity of being* is faulty. They then present themselves as a solution of continuity and are aimed at preserving the true self from annihilation or from the *primitive agonies* that threaten it.'[4]

Let us consider here two types of paradox that are bound up with particular stages in the maturational process. We shall consider, for the first time, the capacity to be alone and the transitional object and phenomena, and, for the second type, the paradoxical defences – the paradox of guilt, that of the fear of breakdown, and paradoxical suicide.

'THE CAPACITY TO BE ALONE' (1958)

The paradox is that the capacity to be alone is based on the experience of being alone in the presence of someone. If we refer to Bertrand Russell's theory of logical types, paradox emerges 'from the confusion of two distinct fields'.[5] Winnicott is able to introduce this paradox because he distinguishes between the subjective experience of inner reality and the experience of external reality, the mother being present. There is, therefore, a confusion between inner reality and outer reality here and paradox makes it possible to make two kinds of reality communicate with one another. This also implies that a process of disillusionment is taking place in the subject; but a psychical space in which paradox might occur has to exist.

# Winnicott and Paradox

The paradox introduced by Winnicott concerning the transitional object is that, according to his definition, the object must be found in order to be created and created in order to be found. That is to say, the environment must facilitate the findings of that object and the child will himself make a creation of that first *'Not-Me' possession*. As Winnicott says, 'My contribution is to ask for a paradox to be accepted and tolerated and respected, and for it not to be resolved. By flight to split off intellectual functioning, it is possible to resolve the paradox, but the price of this is the loss of the value of the paradox itself.'[6] Thus an illusion is necessary if the object is to be well founded, but at the same time 'it is crucial that the object should really exist for the illusion to have any value'.[7] Neither the baby nor the mother, who has an intuition of what is taking place in her relationship with her baby, is aware of a paradox, but Winnicott the observer – and therefore his reader – is. As Roussillon explains:

> 'To accept the paradox of the baby's position with relation to the transitional object as such is to presuppose that one is, as we have said, outside this paradox and at the same time this stage is recognized as a necessary transition, that is to say, that the whole of the illusion-disillusion process is perceived. For this psychical space in which one may place paradoxes is a processual space.'[8]

Winnicott points out[9] that the work of Freud[10] showed how true guilt resided in the intention, in unconscious intention: 'Actual crime is not the cause of guilt-feeling; rather is it the *result* of guilt – guilt that belongs to criminal intention. Only legal guilt refers to a crime; moral guilt refers to inner reality.'[11] We should remember Winnicott's conception of the anti-social tendency, which consists in committing crimes because it still provides some hope of finding contact with others, of finding a solution to conflicts.

'*Fear of breakdown* is both a paradox and a memory of what has not yet happened,' says Roussillon. 'There are moments,' says Winnicott, 'according to my experience, when a patient needs to be told that the breakdown, a fear of which destroys his or her life, *has already been.*'[12]

One might refer here again to paradoxical suicide, a suicide perpetrated in order to avoid being killed, in order to remain in the world of the living. This was the case of a patient who asked him to help her to commit suicide for the *right* reason. Her aim, as Winnicott came to see, was to get it stated by him that she had died in early infancy.

Thus, with this kind of phenomena, the paradoxical response would, according to Winnicott, be to make it possible that something was remembered that had not yet taken place in order to allow it to occur, that is to say, to re-establish a process of maturation that did not take place.

## On certain criticisms made of Winnicott

Here we should like to deal with two criticisms made of Winnicott: that he neglected the role of the father and the Oedipus complex and that his technical variants did not belong to psychoanalysis.

### THE QUESTION OF THE FATHER

As far as the first of these criticisms is concerned, one has to have read Winnicott very superficially to believe that he neglects the role of the father or the Oedipal relationship. Being concerned principally with psychotic patients or with very young children, his attention was drawn to the pre-genital stages: this did not stop him stressing the role of the father from the outset of life and declaring that if the mother did not have a husband to give her support, or if she had not cathected the child's father, the father's psychical development would be affected.

In an adult analysis, like the one recounted in his *Holding and Interpretation*, we see, when we read Winnicott's accounts of the sessions, how hard he tried to bring his patient to triangular relationship. He tried on several occasions to take up the position of the paternal figure in the relationship. For example, he writes:

'In other words, up to this point, which was roughly speaking a year, interrupted by evacuation during terms, the patient's relation to me was an extremely artificial one unless one understands just what was happening. The material was rich and the work done considerable, but it was impossible to reach, for instance, the dynamics of the Oedipus situation. The period of transition was in fact heralded by the patient's first recognition of the reality of jealousy in the external world in the form of a casual statement that he had read something about a thing called the Oedipus complex and didn't hold with it. During his first half of analysis I made no attempt to force the situation because I knew, from the type of the transference, that it would be absolutely futile to do so, and also because the analysis was steadily progressing so that one could expect eventually a development which would throw light on what might be called a resistance or a negative therapeutic reaction.'

Later, Winnicott remarks to the patient that his father is absent from his dreams. The patient then referred to a rivalry that he was then having with a male friend of a female friend. At another moment, still in the same period of analysis, the patient's associations having led him to say that he was not capable of being aggressive, Winnicott told him: 'What you are leading up to is that you have not been able to get to your hate of the man in the triangular relationship.'

At the end of that session, the bell rang and Winnicott had to let in the next patient, who was a man. As the first patient was leaving, 'he implied with his looks that he was enjoying a triangular game, hating a man who was responsible for his being jilted by a girl'. Four days later, the patient remembered incidents in which his father and mother were present and Winnicott remarked, remembering a word from the previous session:

'I picked up the subject of undermining and the interpretation which was appropriate at the time, and showed that it had a present equivalent in castration anxiety, father having turned up at last in theory in the triangular situation which was new. I also linked the end of the last hour with the word "jilt" and with the fact that he heard a man's voice when I let in the next patient after "jilting" him.'

A month later, the patient is able to say that he doesn't like rivalry with men and Winnicott says to him: 'It seems all right to compete when you know you are superior.' The patient replies that he does not like to compete when on unequal terms, to which Winnicott says: 'In the analytic room it is important to you that either we are only two – as when you were a small child with mother – or else when we are three the third is excluded.' There are many such examples. It seems to us to be important to cite a few precise sequences from one of Winnicott's analyses to show that his interpretations do not differ from those of other analysts when the context is the same.

TECHNICAL VARIATIONS

The extension of the field of analysis to borderline cases or psychotics led Winnicott to introduce technical variations into treatment.

Already in 1969, Henri Sauget wrote:

'Winnicott's technical liberties remain within the framework of analytical rigour; they are necessitated by very different psychological structures from those of the classical neuroses. . . . With sometimes necessary variations, analysis can help such subjects to regain a lost equilibrium. This parental or analytical help has nothing to do with spoiling children, which springs from maternal guilt or a reaction formation, just as it has nothing to do with the excessive "softness" of an analyst emerging from a repressed counter-transference. [These variations] demand of the analyst, of his experience, of his human qualities, of his skill, an adaptation to his patient in terms of management. . . . From this point of view Winnicott is unquestionably a rigorous innovator: is not his aim to allow the formation and blossoming of the transference neurosis (or psychosis), the true object of ana-lytical work? The dynamic criterion may justify a variation or a technical modification. The analyst cannot hide behind rigid or ideal technical rules when those rules are implacable to certain patients on account of their unconscious structure. This unconscious structure is ordered by a traumatism that is all the more mutilating in that it occurred so early on in psychical development. That is why it becomes essential to maintain the object relationship even if it must be *outside* the analytic field for a certain length of time and then be brought back to it at a later date.'[13]

Winnicott himself confronted the problem. For him, the essential question was: 'Has the therapist had an analytic training or not?'[14] He emphasizes that psychoanalytical training is the only apprenticeship for a kind of work that is nevertheless not psychoanalysis, especially in the case of child therapy. This is because when the practitioner carries theory inside him, it has become part of himself and he has no need to refer to it consciously.[15]

In his article 'The Aims of Psychoanalytical Treatment', Winnicott writes'

'Analysis for analysis' sake has no meaning for me. I do analysis because that is what the patient needs to have done and to have done with. If the patient does not need analysis then I do something else. . . . [But] if our aim continues to be to verbalize the nascent conscious in terms of the transference then we are practising analysis; if not, then we are analysts practising something else that we deem to be appropriate to the occasion. And why not?'[16]

We can conclude with Henri Sauget: 'Throughout his work Winnicott has remained a lucid practitioner, critical of his practice and careful to have an understanding of it that is based on the heritage of his predecessors.' Hoping that he has given the main outlines of it, he adds that if the reader

'meets on the way obstacles deriving from the complexity of psychical life and from the early source of the disturbances considered, he will always find clinical facts in which the author's authenticity of observation and sincerity will be solid, convincing signposts. It is this that makes his work so attractive, for, aiming to express and to understand the ineffable, he went back to those who were separated by the unintelligible.'

## As he was

Winnicott's biography has been no more than touched on in so far as it was relevant to his work. Now let us turn to what we know of his life in order to grasp his deeper personality and therefore respond perhaps to the question that always crops up: why that particular work and how did Winnicott elaborate it?

Thanks to Clare Winnicott, we have at our disposal an intimate and valuable account of Donald Winnicott's life and character.[17] As has already been said, Donald had a happy childhood in a harmonious family, in which many children lived, played, and worked together. Art and humour played an important role in it.

'There is no doubt that from his earliest years Donald did not doubt that he was loved, and he experienced a security in the Winnicott home which he could take for granted. . . . This capacity *to be at home* served him well throughout his life. There is a pop song which goes "Home is in my heart". That is certainly how Donald experienced it and this gave him an immense freedom which enabled him to feel at home anywhere.'

Many people have attested to this freedom of behaviour, freedom of thought, and freedom of being.[18]

THE GENESIS OF THE VOCATION AND THE WORK

Of course, the profound motivations for a vocation usually remain outside our grasp. However, certain events in Winnicott's childhood and adolescence reveal traits of character, certain tendencies, which are probably not unconnected with his determination to study medicine. At sixteen, a broken collar-bone confined him to the school sick room. It was then that he decided to become a doctor. 'I could see that for the rest of my life I should have to depend on doctors if I damaged myself or became ill, and the only way out of this position was to become a doctor myself.' Perhaps it was this fear of dependence that lay at the origin of Winnicott's *freedom* referred to above.

Later, while training to be a doctor, he became ill with an abscess on the lung and spent three months in a London hospital, in one of those huge old wards that were so familiar to him as a medical student. Donald was highly amused and interested at being lost in a crowd and said, 'I am convinced that every doctor ought to have been once in his life in a hospital bed as a patient.'

His original intention had been to become a country doctor; however, an unexpected encounter, the discovery and reading of one of Freud's books, led him to undergo psychoanalysis. It was the turning point of his life. At the time he was particularly interested in paediatrics and had a post as consultant at Paddington Green Children's Hospital. His work developed side by side with his analysis and gradually turned him from paediatrics to psychoanalysis.

Clare Winnicott notes an interesting detail which says a lot about his contact with children. Almost invariably he gave the child who had been brought to him in consultation something to take away with him, something that 'could afterwards be used and/or destroyed or thrown away'. Donald, she says,

'would quickly reach for a piece of paper and fold it into some shape, usually a dart or a fan, which he might play with for a moment and give to the child as he said goodbye. I never saw this gesture refused by any child. It could be that this simple symbolic act contained the germ of ideas developed in the "Use of an Object" paper written at the end of his life. There could also be a link here with the transitional object concept.'

To return to the genesis of Winnicott's vocation, we should mention the wish for restitution and reparation, which he illustrates very well in an instance reported in his autobiographical note. When he was very young, his sisters had a doll called Rosie and his father teased him about this Rosie, parodying a popular song:

Rosie said to Donald
I love you.
Donald said to Rosie
I don't believe you do.

Donald was exasperated by the voice assumed by his father while singing the song. This doll became more and more unbearable to him and he knew that it would have to be *spoilt* in some way. One day he picked up a croquet mallet and flattened the wax doll's nose. Probably horrified by his action, he felt relieved when his father warmed the wax nose with matches and remoulded it so that the face once more became a face.

'This early demonstration of the restitutive and reparative act certainly made an impression on me, and perhaps made me able to accept the fact that I myself, dear innocent child, had actually become violent directly with a doll, but indirectly with my good-tempered father who was just then entering my conscious life.'

Winnicott did not remember having a transitional object himself, but one day a dream gave him the vague feeling that he had had one and had lost it; this dream experience seemed to him to be so important that he related it (in 1950) in a letter to his wife. Referring to a conversation that he had had with her, he notes:

'Last night I got something quite unexpected, through dreaming, out of what you said. Suddenly you joined up with the nearest thing I could get to my transitional object: it was something I have always known about but I lost the memory of it; at this moment I became conscious of it. There was a very early doll called Lily belonging to my younger sister and I was fond of it, and very distressed when it fell and broke. After Lily I hated *all* dolls. But I always knew that before Lily there was a something of my own. I knew retrospectively that it must have been a doll. But it had never occurred to me that it wasn't just like myself, a person, that is to say it was a kind of other me and a not-me female. And part of me and and yet not, and absolutely inseparable from me. I don't know what happened to it.'

*Winnicott and Paradox*

Clare Winnicott comments: 'Donald never ceased to be in touch with his dream world and to continue his own analysis. It was the deep undercurrent of his life, the orchestral accompaniment to the main theme.'

WINNICOTT AND DEATH

Clare Winnicott relates how she had always encouraged her husband to write his autobiography; he always put it off until later. Yet, in the last years of his life, he began to jot down notes in a notebook, perhaps at the time when 'the reality of his own death had to be negotiated, and this he did, again gradually and in his own way'. 'The title of the autobiography was to be *Not Less than Everything*.'[19] In this notebook he wrote down memories, poems, and an imaginary description of the end of his life in which he describes his lungs filled with water, his heart unable to go on pumping, and asphyxia. 'There had been rehearsals' (he had already had a heart attack). He notes that he had difficulty spelling the word, having left out the *a*, because, he says, it contains the word 'hearse'. He imagines himself dead. He remembers his friends who had died during the First World War and the sense that he had always had that his being alive was 'a facet of one thing of which their deaths can be seen as other facets'. It is difficult, he says, for a man to die 'without a son to imaginatively kill and to survive him'. This, for him, was the only continuity that men know, while women are continuous. And he refers to King Lear and his relationship with his daughters, especially with the youngest one, who should have been a boy.

He was constantly playing with inner and outer reality: 'This', Clare Winnicott says, 'makes reality bearable to the individual, so that denial can be avoided and the experience of living can be as fully realized as possible. In his own words "playing can be said to reach its own saturation point, which refers to the capacity to contain experience".'[20]

As ever, avid for experience, Donald 'would have hated to miss the inner experience of the reality of his own death, and he imaginatively achieved that experience'. Was not this indeed a way of trying to get himself and her accustomed to the idea that it would come?

As their correspondence abundantly shows, each was indispensable to the other's work. But they were bound together not only by their work, but also by other interests, especially their friends and art, which for them were 'the prerequisite for creative living'. This is illustrated in a moving dream that Clare Winnicott had a few years after her husband's death:

'I dreamt that we were in our favourite shop in London, where there is a circular staircase to all floors. We were running up and down these stairs, grabbing things from here, there, and everywhere as Christmas presents for our friends. We were really having a spending spree, knowing that as usual we would end up keeping many of the things ourselves. I suddenly realized that Donald was alive after all and I thought with relief, "Now I shan't have to worry about the Christmas card." Then we were sitting in the restaurant having our morning coffee as usual (in fact we always went out to morning coffee on Saturday). We were facing each other, elbows on the table, and I looked at him full in the face and said: "Donald there's something we have to say to each other, some truth that we have to say, what is it?" With his very blue eyes looking unflinchingly into mine, he said: "That this is a dream." I replied slowly: "Oh yes, of course, you died, you died a year ago." He reiterated my words: "Yes, I died a year ago."'

Living on in Clare's thoughts, Winnicott also remains for those who love him and admire him. We are reminded of this prayer jotted down in his notebook:

'Oh God! May I be alive when I die.'

Clare Winnicott died on 17 April 1984 while the French edition of this book was being printed.

She gave us unstinting encouragement throughout its writing. She liked the title; she took the trouble to find a squiggle that she thought appropriate because it shows its author's sense of humour and skill at the squiggle. Furthermore, this squiggle[21] bears a title in Donald Winnicott's hand, which is rare.

In one of her last letters she said how delighted she was to learn that the book was finished and sent us her 'affectionate greetings and happy thoughts about your book'.

# Interviews

## Introduction to the interviews

Winnicott was in turn ignored, criticized, rejected, admired by his British colleagues, but in the end came to occupy what we regard as his true place, that of a subtle, perceptive clinician and original researcher.

We wanted to know how, today, Winnicott's work is regarded by French psychoanalysts and we asked some of them whether their various activities, whether they treated neuroses or psychoses, adults or children, had had an effect on the way they confronted Winnicott's work.

We thus tried to assess the *present* impact of Winnicott on all those who are interested in the psychology of the adult and of the child, and in psychoanalysis.

The following agreed to be interviewed:

**Jean-Marc Alby**,
Professor, Department of Psychiatry and Medical Psychology, Faculté de Médecine Saint-Antoine, Paris.

**Raymond Cahn**,
Director of the Hôpital de jour du Parc Montsouris (CEREP), Member of the Société psychanalytique de Paris.

**René Diatkine,**
Member of the Société psychanalytique de Paris.

**André Green,**
Former Director of the Institut de Psychanalyse de Paris.
Former professor at University College, London (Freud Memorial Chair).

**Evelyn Kestemberg,**
Psychoanalyst. Director of the Centre de psychanalyse et psychothérapie du XIII$^e$ arrondissement de Paris.

**Serge Lebovici,**
Professor of Child Psychiatry, Université de Paris XIII.

**Jean-Bertrand Pontalis,**
Member of the Association psychanalytique de France.
Director of the *Nouvelle Revue de Psychanalyse*.

**Daniel Widlöcher,**
Professor of psychiatry, Université de Paris VI.
Former President of the Fédération européenne de psychanalyse.

## Being English and a psychoanalyst
## Interview with Jean-Marc Alby

*Jean-Marc Alby*:   My first meeting with Winnicott took place at an International Congress of Psychoanalysis at Copenhagen. In a small group, Winnicott was recounting, with all his vitality and veracity, his consultation with a Finnish boy whom he had been asked to see during a tour of Finland. This child, who had been hospitalized in the orthopaedic department of a children's hospital, presented certain symptoms of a vague kind, including messing, headaches, and abdominal pains. There was no urgent symptom to justify recourse to a psychotherapist.[1]

He spoke no English and Winnicott did not know Finnish. Winnicott picked up a sheet of paper and began to scribble: a relationship was then established with the child, who began to project his own personality, dreams, and anxieties into the drawing. In this way Winnicott was able to assess the child's difficulties.

Later, during Anglo-French psychoanalytical meetings, I realized, paradoxically through Michael and Enid Balint, how important Winnicott was: Winnicott had been a paediatrician, Balint's father a doctor. I was able to identify with them in this medical connection; intellectual complicity with Winnicott is often marked by interlinked paths.

*Anne Clancier:* Were you already interested in paediatrics and child psychoanalysis?

*J-MA:* Yes, I had already been involved with paediatrics and child psychiatry. One thing sticks out in my memory: as an intern at a paediatric consultation I saw paediatricians take the hand of an infant and gently hold it. It is one of the gestures that reading Winnicott reminds me of all the time: the physical contact, the informal relationship between this bundle of flesh, the mother, and the paediatrician – I was very moved by that.

*AC:* Yes, paediatricians often have intuitions about infants' needs. I remember how in the 1930s, long before psychoanalysts had advocated physical and emotional contacts with babies, Dr Lere Boullet, in his hospital paediatrics department asked both externs and interns to take the babies out for walks into the hospital courtyards, saying: 'Can't you see those children are bored. You must look after them, take them out for walks.' Some of the students laughed. But that paediatrician was right, because those children, deprived of contact with their mothers during their hospitalization and separated from them, perhaps for the first time, needed those contacts. It helped them to cure their somatic disturbances.

*J-MA:* Yes, I feel completely on Winnicott's side on this – like when he allows us to share in his observation of a child in a 'set situation'. From the theoretical point of view, what interests me – and where I found him most helpful – is his concept of the transitional object and the field of illusion. When he speaks of the false self, however, I find him much more difficult to follow.

*AC:* You mentioned Balint in relation to Winnicott. Do you

think the Hungarian school played a role in the formation of
Winnicott's thinking?

*J-MA*:   One may well think of Ferenczi and his active technique. When Winnicott speaks about the value of the body, of
breathing, of relaxation, of being and at the way of being in
one's body, he raises the question of the self that is or is not in
the body at certain times. The body and the self link him to
Ferenczi and to Balint. On this matter, I would mention the
psychoanalyst's 'presence', as Sacha Nacht did, when we
remember that Winnicott, when with a very 'regressed'
patient, a borderline case, always had a glass of water nearby,
in case she felt she needed it.

I would like to talk to you about the touchstone of every
therapeutic relationship: the counter-transference. In
teaching, in the groups, in the case studies, does one not aim
at helping the future psychiatrist, the doctor, to become
aware of his counter-attitudes?[2]

To return to his work with children, what greatly impressed
me in Winnicott, in his assessments, was the way he took into
account the child's infirmities in his development and his
relationships with the environment. This testified very much
to Winnicott the paediatrician.

On the subject of the environment, he might have been
accused of naivety; in fact, Winnicott was far from being
naive. He certainly knew what a good-enough environment
was, he knew what people were, how profoundly ambivalent
they were. He reminded me very much of a character I am
very fond of, Father Brown, the priest-detective hero of G. K.
Chesterton, who, like Graham Greene, was very fond of
detective stories. While appearing to be utterly innocent,
Father Brown solves the most complicated riddles. His
innocence is only apparent and is used by the character as a
weapon. He has a sense of human understanding; he is
self-effacing, a believer in grace,[3] an order beyond situations
and conflicts: his power lay in that 'naive' certainty.
Chesterton's idealistic and religious convictions won
through. His conception of human relations reminded me
strongly of Winnicott.

*AC*:   When you describe this individual, one might imagine him to be some kind of idealist, but perhaps above all he was someone who allowed his unconscious to function, who knew how to identify with others at a deep level. These are indispensable qualities for a psychoanalyst and ones that Winnicott possessed to the highest degree.

What do you think of the transitional object, of the transitional area, particularly where creativity is concerned? Isn't it very important in clinical medicine, because, after all, one often sees patients who, when things get better, are capable of creative activity?

*J-MA*:   Winnicott is right: there is something of the order of illusion in all psychical reality, but why attach so much importance to this field of illusion? It is a rather too Platonic conception for my taste.

*AC*:   It is true that he uses the word illusion in order to be able to say dis-illusion and dis-illusionment. The field of illusion is a creative field because, at a given moment, it makes it possible to move to a domain which is that of the mother who knows, because she is good enough, at what moment to frustrate the infant and to force him to confront opposition thanks to her aggressive movement.

*J-MA*:   You are quite right to remind me of Winnicott's concern for the dynamics of development. Before him, Freud had denounced that same illusion in *Mass Psychology and the Analysis of the Ego*, since every feeling of love was essentially illusion. This brings us to the question of the reality of the sense of self. Is it not all mere reflexion? Is there a living reality?

*AC*:   Winnicott speaks of the incommunicable kernel, that is to say, the silent kernel of the personality that is not necessarily an illusion, but incommunicable.

*J-MA*:   That is a useful notion.

*AC*:   One might refer here to Freud's view of what might be included under the heading of illusions, religion, for example, and art. When he speaks of art he seems to be saying that it is a good illusion – doesn't this amount to saying that in creation one rediscovers good internal objects and gives them to others, thus rediscovering communication with them? It belongs to the order of love, it is libidinal.

*J-MA*:   Analysts tend too often to interpret everything in terms of defence: Winnicott dealt severely with this will to reduce. Furthermore we may have doubts as to our capacity to intervene in the pre-Oedipal period, which is experienced in an ineffable manner, perhaps re-experienced during analysis in the same way, without any possible interpretation, whereas what concerns the Oedipal conflict may be elaborated more easily in verbal terms, the 'as if'. You will find an echo of these themes in Reik, in the place he gives to intuition: interpretation counts for less than the capacity for identification.

In Winnicott, the absence of systematization and the pragmatism are closely bound up, for me, with the English mentality. It reminds me of Locke. In his *Treatise on Education*, you will find the same mentality: absence of systematization, pragmatism, a sense of fantasy. Someone else who would be in good company with Winnicott is Lewis Carroll.

*AC*:   Yes, there is even a point in common on a biographical level between Lewis Carroll and Winnicott: both were the only boy in a family surrounded by several sisters.

*J-MA*:   But there is also the playful use of nonsense.

*AC*:   Yes, and one finds Shakespeare, who, in poetic formulas, gives us dazzling insights into the human psyche.

*J-MA*:   I have also been very susceptible to an attitude in Winnicott that I might dare to call 'goodness'. But, since that might be misunderstood, let us call it openness to others, a profound availability to others' needs.

*AC*:   Might one not say receptiveness, empathy? One should also remember his capacity to give or receive criticism, while preserving a respect for the other person, and his tolerance. We know that when there were tensions in the British psychoanalytic world, between the groups that had formed around Anna Freud and Melanie Klein. Winnicott belonged to the 'middle group' and acted as conciliator. As he said, he took from each side those theoretical elements that suited him, which he considered useful in his clinical practice.

*J-MA*:   I liked his modesty, too; he did not believe himself to be omnipotent with his patients. He did not ask of them what they were not capable of giving. Thus he did not expect mothers to be very good or even good, but simply good enough; he sustained those who had difficulties with their children, telling them to do at least what they could, whereas Freud said that whatever mothers do it will be bad in any case.

A very important point, common to Winnicott and Balint, is their conviction that the patient 'cures his doctor'.[4]

To end, I would like to draw attention to Winnicott's love of paradox, which is suggested in the title of your book. Winnicott loved to be paradoxical, in the manner of many English thinkers, if one includes in it a sense of humour and respect for others.

## A rebel
## Interview with Raymond Cahn

*Raymond Cahn*: Reading the first of Winnicott's books to appear in France was a shock to me: hitherto I had looked at, listened to, reacted to patients with borderline 'as if', or psychotic structures quite differently.

On another plane, my understanding of what was really therapeutic in the Hôpital de jour pour adolescents [the CEREP], of which I am director, really came about only after contact with Winnicott's work.

*Anne Clancier*: Did you actually work with Winnicott and, if so, what did this bring to the members of the team?

*RC*: Yes, we worked in a team with Winnicott. What, at the time, we called transitional space and time, with the different notions that this implies, was important from the outset in our work together and our understanding of it.

*AC*: Was it quickly integrated into the work of the medical team?

*RC*: What now seems quite obvious to us may not have been taken into account at first by all the medical staff involved; it is still difficult to assess.

In medical institutions we are in the habit of considering that transitional space is situated at the level of the traditional institutional areas, whether creativity, conversation, workshop activity, including indeed school activity, in so far as it belongs to an open pedagogy, one involving mutual discovery and dialogue. But it seemed to me that the transitional space was the very tissue of institutional life, far more than the settings that organized it. In conflicts, as in the ordinary situations of life, as soon as a dialogue is established leading to an explanation of what is happening there in the everyday setting, a true dialogue may occur in which the adolescent experiences a sense both of being recognized and of being able to formulate something that he had not previously been aware of. At the time when I am giving expression to this, it seems to me so obvious that it is difficult to see its specificity from the Winnicottian point of view. One is caught up in an intangible register in which the quality of listening and dialogue is far more important than what one can actually say about it in an abstract way.

AC: But that is precisely Winnicott's contribution – he altered the quality of our listening and dialogue. Something is transformed that is not quite like what takes place in analysis.

RC: Indeed, in our institution, for example, we might talk quietly about things and try to elaborate them gradually so that they begin to look like the truth and are taken in by the adolescent. This correct way of speaking of things seems to me to be more therapeutic than deep interpretations or more or less psychoanalytic interventions, which should only take place in a psychotherapeutic setting.

AC: This may be compared with what takes place in a family. I know young couples who have read the transcripts of Winnicott's broadcasts for the BBC. Without any intervention on the part of the therapist, something changes in the family atmosphere.

RC: This is because Winnicott gave pre-eminence to something that takes place at the level of the human being (*l'être*), as opposed to something less than human (*un moins être*), or a splitting that would prevent the human being from emerging. So you see one can make much greater use of Winnicott's work than if one integrates it into classical psychoanalysis.

AC: Your term '*un moins être*' is interesting: it is not generally used by psychoanalysts.

RC: There's a trace there of my own friendship with Georges Amado, who devoted a whole chapter to Winnicott in his book *De l'enfant à l'adulte. La psychanalyse au regard de l'être.*

*AC*: It strikes me that there is a close similarity between this conception of the human being, of *l'etre*, and Winnicott's concept of the self. Authentic being seems to be the self and this enables us to understand the Winnicottian notion of the false self. What do you think?

*RC*: What bothers me in Winnicott's notion of the false self is the use made of it by the anti-psychiatrists, notably Laing. It seems that for them, the false self is that of the normal person and that the psychotic expresses his true being through his psychosis. This is a distortion of Winnicott's concept. When Winnicott speaks of the secret ego, he is not speaking of the psychotic ego.

One point was of great interest to us in our hospital: the dimension of the subjective object, something that comes into play before the object relation and which presupposes that one is in the primary narcissistic zone, let us call it the pre-object zone, in which there is an absence of differentiation. The traces of what might take place there are repeated in the therapist's induced counter-attitudes, whether they take the form of hate or hyper-concern.

*AC*: That is interesting. Is this your own hypothesis?

*RC*: Yes and no. Winnicott took it up in the famous example he gave in *Playing and Reality*: with one patient, he suddenly had a sort of purely counter-transferential intuition, which was in no way linked to the material that his patient had brought him.

*AC*: When he said to the patient: 'I know perfectly well that you are a man, but what I am listening to is a girl . . .'

*RC*: Yes, there are certain eruptions of affects tinged with irrationality, then. They seem extremely archaic and are induced by something prior to what, subsequently, is to constitute the object relation.

*AC*: This subjective object seems to be a sort of pre-object, as some psychoanalysts call it, the origin of what is later to become the object.

*RC*: It is not yet an object because it is part of the subjective area, that is to say, it is created by the child and it is not regarded as alien, outside himself and desired.

113

*AC*: Would it be the moment when the child finds the transitional object?

*RC*: Before this it already has to have occurred to him to find the transitional object. In his book *Playing and Reality*, Winnicott concludes that there is a stage in the development of the human being prior to the possibility of recognizing external reality. In the 'tailpiece' to that work he stresses the 'conception-perception gap': this is a crucial key in understanding Winnicott.

His work does not constitute a well-structured, well-organized – I was going to say French – theoretical system. It is much more than that: an extraordinarily new insight, with theoretical neologisms, neo-concepts maintaining together things that apparently, on the level of the secondary processes, are not compatible. This is a stroke of genius, because at the same time it speaks to us at the secondary level and resonates inside us at other levels.

*AC*: Isn't this a paradox? And, of course, paradox is a fundamental notion for Winnicott.

*RC*: It links fascination with what is imperceptible and a specificity that cannot be integrated into other theories.

*AC*: It is easy to see how people who are too Cartesian, too rationalistic, cannot appreciate Winnicott. There is that pragmatic side of the Anglo-Saxons and the same love of nonsense that one finds in Lewis Carroll, for example, who, as you know, was a mathematician as well as a writer.

*RC*: Yes. I would like to talk to you about a piece of work that we have done with phoniatric colleagues, all of whom have undergone psychotherapy themselves. They were confronted with technical problems that they could not resolve. The children with whom they were dealing were all, to a greater or lesser degree, retarded in their speech. The structures were difficult to locate in so far as I had not myself seen these children: but it seemed that the disturbances ranged from severe neurotic difficulties to pre-psychotic states, in which the symptom took the form of an inability to express oneself in a symbolic register.

We had done an elaboration together of a Winnicottian type, a technical approach that was much more an approach of accompaniment, of exchange of a corporal, ludic type, verbalized by the adult whose look gave the child a status, a recognition that he had not had: by anamnesis we were made aware of the extent to which this had been lacking for the child. Those games in which there was never any interpretation, because I didn't want those colleagues who were not analysts to conduct a 'wild' analysis, were incredibly effective.

*AC*: Were they in fact close to the squiggle method?

*RC*: Yes, but we used anything, any object in the environment, including electric plugs, taps, the drum and the rocking-horse that were in the room. We set up a sort of game between two people that renewed a series of discoveries and of control of the present/absent object, formulated verbally in the presence of the therapist.

I saw Winnicott shortly before his death, at the Congress of Child Psychiatry at Edinburgh. I was fascinated by his face, by a sort of light that radiated from it.

*AC*: Something quite fundamental in his personality seems to me to be bound up with the fact that Winnicott was a paediatrician before becoming a psychoanalyst. What do you think?

*RC*: Precisely. I nearly forgot to tell you about that. It is in fact quite fundamental. I, too, was a paediatrician before becoming a psychoanalyst and I believe that this gives us a special approach.

*AC*: I have a view of my own on this matter. I believe that it is necessary that all psychoanalysts should have the opportunity of working for at least a year with infants, either in a crèche, a hospital, a kindergarten, it doesn't matter, but that they should have a good knowledge of infants and be able to observe them and play with them.

*RC*: I entirely agree. It would be especially necessary for men, for in that contact with infants there is something of a maternal relationship that men cannot experience. That struck me as very important when I was doing paediatrics. I don't think it is neurotic.

*AC*: On the contrary, it would be neurotic to refuse that dimension, which Winnicott possessed.

*RC:* Everything that Winnicott wrote on the adolescent seems to me to be very important, too, as well as what he wrote about early development, mainly that parents must be killed, but never die. That's a truth we have to learn to live with.

*AC:* One can understand this through the transitional object, which is bitten, pummelled, soiled, attacked, but whose contact and smell the infant loves, though it must not be washed and lasts for years. Perhaps adolescents relive that, too, with their parents, when they are going through rebellious periods with them?

*RC:* That strikes me as an essential dimension of therapy: to be constantly attacked, challenged, rejected, but to remain alive and available, that is what Winnicott calls the survival of the analyst.

*AC:* Yes, the patient, like the adolescent, rejects and introjects at the same time.

*RC:* I would like to stress again what Winnicott has contributed to the understanding and treatment of psychosis.

*AC:* I often get the impression that colleagues who have dealt neither with children, nor with psychotics, have difficulty understanding Winnicott's thought.

*RC:* Yes, the whole of Freudian theory sets out from something that already exists; Winnicott, on the other hand, felt that something must be constituted for the psychical functioning to be able to be established and developed. He sets out from the immediacy of the relationship.

To conclude, I would say that Winnicott is a rebel who, intuitively and very simply, incorporated analysis into a much wider, inter-human process. Psychoanalysis has a vocation and an imperative to be imperialistic for everything concerning interrelationships and psychotherapy. Now Winnicott arrived at this paradox of going beyond, that is to say, integrating psychoanalysis into a dimension that included it in turn – that of the shared game: that is one of his many paradoxes.

# A great open-mindedness
## Interview with René Diatkine

*Anne Clancier*:   You have long experience of child psychoanalysis, so I would like to ask you what, in your opinion,
Winnicott contributed to this area.

*René Diatkine*:   We owe to Winnicott a large number of notions
that have given us a glimpse of what lay hidden behind the
obscurity of the established concepts. Unfortunately, strik-
ingly new ideas are very soon 'reified' by those lacking his
inventive genius. This has happened in the case of the 'transitional' objects or spaces. Winnicott brought out in a most
impressive way that beside what was dramatically internal or
external, there was a field of cathexes and activities for which
the question did not arise. Nowadays the 'transitional objects'
have become a sort of hold-all for less original minds.

*AC*:   What do you think of Winnicott's words, 'There's no such
thing as an infant'?

*RD*:   This is one of his most felicitous statements and the whole
development of studies concerning the interaction between
the baby and his mother, the baby and his environment, have
since validated his aphorism. Nowadays we see everything
that was not seen either by the genetic psychologists working
in their laboratories, or by our late-lamented René Spitz. The
baby's crying, the first communication, the transformation of
babbling into the beginnings of language are incomprehensi-
ble if one does not take the environment into account. How
the mother responds, stimulates, calms, allows herself to be
transformed into a mother, are the essential givens in any
understanding of the epigenesis of the psyche. Winnicott
showed that all this is possible only in terms of 'primary
maternal concern'. Even if one may now modify this brilliant
description of mothers' deep attitudes at the moment of the
child's birth, it is a notion that has transformed our under-
sanding of the effect of the mother's desires on the child.
Nevertheless Winnicott's aphorism poses a difficult question
to psychoanalytic theory. Psychoanalysis confronts mental
functioning from the point of view of the individual's solitude, from the patient's capacity – whether he is a child or an
adult – to construct the transference. Mother and father are

imagos elaborated on the basis of the child's successive experiences, experiences in which mother and father have played an essential role by their presence and absence, but also many other external and intra-psychical elements. The parents' fantasies and the mother's illusion are as difficult to integrate into a coherent metapsychological view as the concept of interaction. But others, before Winnicott, including the Anna Freud school, with its notion of 'real objects', or Margaret Mahler, with her notion of symbiosis, came up against the same difficulties.

*AC*: Winnicott had many ideas, most of them extremely fruitful, but when one tries to grasp his concepts, it is often very difficult to do so.

*RD*: The most striking formulas are not necessarily positions based on the most rigorous epistemology, but discovery often disappears beneath the pitiless blows of logic.

*AC*: Can one be Winnicottian in child analysis?

*RD*: For a long time, thank God, Winnicott was not a Winnicottian. I don't really know what the term means. There can hardly be a school of open-mindedness. The fact that the words or techniques of an inventive psychoanalyst are parroted by people devoid of any imagination is rather sad. The squiggle is not a technique, but a wonderful example of creation, caught on the spot, which is interesting only by virtue of Winnicott's conscious and unconscious associations and counter-attitudes. It was said that patients regressed on his couch and he often repeated that opinion of others. Was this a special tendency in his way of analysing adults? Probably, but above all it was a way of understanding the psychoanalytic process in both adult and child. Winnicott's interventions are highly interesting. They often take a psychodramatic turn quite capable of mobilizing the child. And it is on this matter that it is not easy to draw a distinction between child psychoanalysis and psychotherapy. Are we to call the treatment of the Piggle psychoanalysis? The question remains open.

*AC*: I recently heard a colleague say: Winnicott was a theoretician, whereas Melanie Klein was a clinician. What do you think?

*RD*:  Both saw what others did not see, though both Melanie Klein and Winnicott lacked epistemological rigour. Both elaborated theories, pretty lame ones, like all psychoanalytic theories. It is left to us to decide how best to use others' theories – it isn't very easy. I find any system that explains everything in advance disturbing, for it leaves out the element of surprise. Any concept invoked to hide poverty of thought, as I said earlier, is badly used. And today this is what usually happens to Winnicott's concepts. Many of them are wonderful clinical descriptions (like primary maternal concern, the infant's capacity to be alone with his mother). There, too, theoretical elaboration is difficult. Nevertheless it is necessary if we are to avoid falling into a psychological realism that denatures the experience of which discourse ought to take account.

## Winnicott and the model of the environment
## Interview with André Green

*André Green*:  I saw Winnicott for the first time at an international congress of psychoanalysis at Edinburgh in 1961. During the days prior to the congress a pre-congress had taken place in London during which the British psychoanalysts had organized small working groups with foreign colleagues to enable them to gain a better awareness of how the British psychoanalysts worked. In these groups, which were made up of fifteen or so individuals, there was a presentation of clinical material, followed by a discussion. I chose Winnicott's group, because I already knew something of his work. I had heard him four years before, in 1957, at the Paris Congress. He had read a paper on regression and withdrawal that I found very striking, but I had not seen him in action, so to speak, until London, during that little seminar, where I heard him speak for the first time of the squiggle technique. I was greatly struck by the man. Indeed Winnicott's originality of thought and his originality as a person were inseparable: his authenticity, the direct nature of his human contacts, the way in which he immediately became involved in the material that he was presenting. Later I met Winnicott at other conferences, notably in Amsterdam in 1965, and I was able to speak to him, but I can make no claim to Winnicott's friendship in the way that a number of his British colleagues can.

There was a long latency period in my relations with Winnicott's work. On my return from Edinburgh, I did not rush to read Winnicott's works. I was still in my period of commenting on Freud and was very interested in Lacan's work.

I really began to feel close to Winnicott in 1972–73. The report that I delivered in London at the International Psychoanalytical Conference in 1975 was dedicated to Winnicott's memory. May I remind you of the circumstances of that report? I had been asked to present a point of view that was to draw up the changes that had occurred in psychoanalytic theory and practice. I was then struck by the fact that ideas that are now entirely accepted among us were defended by Winnicott as early as 1954. Winnicott belongs to a movement within the British school that has been strongly influenced by Melanie Klein, but had taken its distance in relation to her theories. A great deal has been made of the fact that Winnicott was first of all a paediatrician and that paediatrics had influenced his view of psychoanalysis. This is true only up to a point. Of course, Winnicott had an exceptional intuition of what was happening inside the child – his therapeutic consultations provide wonderful examples of this. We have seen how, in so short a time, he was capable of understanding the most important things. What I mean is that if Winnicott saw children as he did see them, if he listened to them as he did, if he had so intuitive and deep an insight into them, it was not simply because he was a paediatrician, but because he had undergone psychoanalysis as an adult: it was, therefore, his experience of psychoanalysis, which was prolonged and repeated several times indeed, that enabled him to see the child with the eyes of the analysed adult who has rediscovered the child in himself, with all his vulnerability and creativity. The child that he sees is not a psychoanalytic child who might appear to an adult with no preconceptions.

If today I was trying to assess Winnicott's importance, I

would say that in psychoanalysis, after Freud, I see two authors who have pushed their research and coherence very far on the basis of two quite different points of view, and which up to a certain point converge. Those two authors are Lacan and Winnicott.

The link may seem surprising, but in the end not so much, for it turns out that some of Lacan's disciples, who ten years ago were still strictly orthodox in relation to Lacanian theory, have evolved in Winnicott's direction. The parallel has already been made.

Why is there a parallel? The interest that Lacan accorded to language, to speech, dates from his 1953 report. Notice how close the dates are, since I have just alluded to an article by Winnicott of 1954. Lacan sets out from a position that seems to me well-grounded, but the conclusions that he draws from it seem to me today to be unacceptable, whereas the initial questioning strikes me as of crucial importance. There was on Freud's part a deliberate choice that psychoanalysis should be a treatment that worked exclusively through speech, through verbal exchange, and that it should manage to deprive itself of any other means. But can one make the leap from the fact that it is a 'talking treatment' to the notion that the unconscious is structured like a language?

Lacan found an answer which for my part I do not share, though I found it attractive for a time – though as early as 1960 I began to criticize it. I shall not resume the critique that I have developed elsewhere, but I would stress that the crucial question of psychoanalysis remains: how is it that by means of speech we change something in the structure of the subject, whereas what we change does not belong to the field of speech? Indeed Lacan himself has evolved on this matter, since he had to introduce the concept of *lalangue*, the maternal *lalangue*.

Winnicott tackles the question in a different way, in a way that seems even more fruitful than Lacan's. Before Winnicott there was no psychoanalytic theory of the environment, or 'set-up', to use Winnicott's own term. I did tackle the question and showed, I think, that the model of the dream and the model of the environment are homogeneous models. Freud

*Winnicott and Paradox*

never explained his position on this, never provided a theory of the environment. He considered that the various ways of practising psychoanalysis were a set of practical, 'facilitating' measures, but did not seek to discover what they referred to. The interest that he attached to applied psychoanalysis showed very clearly that he did not intend to restrict psychoanalysis to psychoanalytic practice. Nevertheless psychoanalytic practice is the privileged access to the unconscious, which one can see at work, with a greater or lesser degree of precision, in any other context, literary, aesthetic, or social phenomena, for example.

In fact, Winnicott poses an epistemological notion of the first importance, the notion that the discoveries of a discipline are related to the means that they assume and that other means would produce other results. It should be noted that Winnicott was well aware of the limitations of psychoanalysis. He said that when he was able to practise psychoanalysis he did so, but that when he was not, for reasons connected, for example, to the patient's psychical structure or to the function of certain material circumstances he used something other than psychoanalysis. This initial position really amounts to a questioning of what psychoanalytic method represents, of the nature of the metaphor that is capable of working something and of discovering something on the basis of that metaphor, which is behind the method. It is obvious that in Winnicott it is not the model of the dream that is given primacy, but the model of maternal care. If one had to attempt a systematization of Winnicott's discoveries, one would have to say that it is on the basis of the model of the set-up that the field of the intermediate area, the area of illusion, of the analyst as transitional object, of the relations between analysis and playing, of the relations between the I and playing open up. There then opens up a category of thought that is quite extraordinary, namely, paradoxical thought. On several occasions, Winnicott says that it is a paradox and that one must above all not try to resolve it.

So we must remain in this fruitful ambiguity proposed by Winnicott. Paradoxical thought, characterized by a suspension of judgements on life, a suspension that decrees that for once, for a certain field, one has no need to pronounce judgement to know whether it was created or found because it was already there; one has no need to pronounce judgement to know whether it is inside or outside, because it is on the frontier, although it should be specified that Winnicott did say that for a transitional object to be established there must previously have been an established internal object. It is a homage that he pays in passing to Melanie Klein, but, in my opinion, he goes farther, some would say in a different direction, than Melanie Klein.

This approach of Winnicott's through judgement, through the suspension of judgement, is something that is absolutely indispensable when we are dealing with borderline cases. What one calls reality, which is a heavy concept, difficult to handle, might certainly benefit from such an approach. Freud said in one of his articles on psychosis that reality is represented in the psyche by the ideas and judgements that have been made of it. Here we are in a field of infinite perspective, in so far as the so-called notion of the repression of reality, a rather old-fashioned notion, does not teach us a great deal; but if one approaches this question from the side of the border between inside and outside, of the intermediate area as an area of intersection, between the outside and the inside, in which the problems of impingement, intrusion, separation, abandonment come into play, at the frontiers of the subject's possibilities, one can understand the importance of Winnicott's thought without attaching to the anecdotal aspect of the transitional object, which is of course something that has its own value, but has above all an interest in so far as it refers to the space of which it forms part and to the time when it begins to function.

I believe that, generally speaking, the very notion of transitionality is interesting and one that may be used even outside the context in which Winnicott uses it. For example, it might be extended to the notion of conflict, an essential Freudian position. I believe that whenever there is antagonism, with the domination of one term over another, an alternative and oscillating domination, the excluded term tends to return, to reoccupy the space; consequently, it is possible, as in any area of movement, to imagine a no-man's-land, where the metaphor would assume a meeting in the potential reunion of what has been separated.

However, I am not an unconditional Winnicottian, if only because the problems posed by Lacan have interested me, for an analyst who really wants to think about practice cannot dispense with a reflection upon language, a reflection that is absent in Winnicott.

Winnicott has been criticized for neglecting infantile sexuality. That is undeniable, not that I believe that what Winnicott describes is outside the field of infantile sexuality, but that sexuality is not named or it is so in a very restrictive way. Winnicott believes, and it is an interesting idea, that there can be no idea before there is an ego to recognize the fact. What we have here is a sort of matrix of the ego, a matricial ego, an original ego. It is an ego that is not differentiated from the id. Obviously, it is only from the moment that a differentiated ego exists that the id can take on an individuality.

I believe that genetic conceptions, historical conceptions are not without their inconvenience, because they force us to simplify problems, that it would be much better to speak in structural terms and at that moment to consider that sexuality is on the one hand everywhere, at the level of time, but nothing eludes it, and that the property of sexuality is precisely to see something erected before it: the anti-sexual, which Freud called towards the end of his life the destruction drive. One may or may not be in agreement with the theory of the death instinct. What is obvious is that where there is sexuality there is sexual conflict. One may vary one's positions, as Freud certainly did, on the nature of this anti-sexual factor, but it is very important to take it into consideration from the *polemical* point of view of original conflict.

On Winnicott's side, there is a 'forgetting' (forgetting in the sense understood by the Greeks) of the sexual, a distraction from the sexual. However I believe that Winnicott is speaking to us of sexuality even if he does not name it. He tells us so many things, particularly about the so-called anti-sexual factors. There is in Winnicott the embryo of a conception of negativity, to which I am very attached. In particular, there is what Winnicott calls the negative aspect of relationships in the note added in 1971 to his article on transitional objects and phenomena. He says that, for certain patients, the thing that is not there is more important than the thing that is; it is the only real thing, whether or not the thing is there later.

I forgot to say something to you more particularly about my personal experience of Winnicott: I did not discover him, I encountered him. That is to say, I was myself already engaged in a certain line of research when I read Winnicott. I then said to myself: that's exactly what I think. Indeed in certain cases I had actually written things that were fairly close to what Winnicott himself had written. It was not, therefore, a discovery, but a meeting. Over the years I have undertaken an exegesis of Freud and for years and years I tried above all to understand what he meant, then I realized that in modern clinical psychoanalysis what Freud said did not accord with what one saw in the analyses of difficult patients, whereas it worked perfectly in cases of hysterical or obsessional neurosis. It was necessary, therefore, to work out a theory of these new facts in an epistemology that belonged to our time, our experience, with references that were not those that dominated Freud's epistemological horizon. Of course Freud pushed back the limits of that horizon, he carried out a revolution, but nevertheless he was in a sense the prisoner of that horizon.

Now today, in my opinion, there is a whole revaluation of the clinical field that does not consist in adopting, in adding borderline structures to what we already know. It is rather a recentring; in other words, neurosis is no longer at the centre of our preoccupations, not that it has disappeared, but the interest of the borderline cases is that they constitute the ideal promontory from which one may observe both the side of neurosis and the side of psychosis – though it is fairly difficult to distinguish what the borderline cases are and almost impossible to do so in the case of the psychoses. Freud did provide us with valuable suggestions concerning the psychoses, but they cannot be of any use to us either in theory or in clinical work.

I believe that if Winnicott is, in every respect, the analyst of the borderline cases, he is at the frontier of theory and practice. The concept of the border is quite central to his thinking, since it is an area of intersection; it seems to me, therefore, an interesting direction to take, though not of course exclusively.

I have also been interested in Bion because Bion's Kleinism seems to me to be a neo-Kleinism, with a return to Freud that reintegrated the past. For me, Bion and Winnicott are fairly close, not only because the *container* and *holding* are notions that may refer to similar things, but because there is, in both Winnicott and Bion, a wish to think in new, original terms and to try to think out certain patients' mental structures.

Winnicott seems to me, then, at the crossroads of several new theoretical reflections. But he is the man with whom one wishes to travel part of the way because he combines his humanity with a marvellous capacity to astonish us at the very heart of what seems familiar.

## A yeast for thought
## Interview with Evelyne Kestemberg

*Evelyne Kestemberg*:   I must have met Winnicott in London in the 1950s. At first I took him to be one of those original Englishmen, attractive by their eccentricity, but not very serious. Later I heard him give a lecture to the Société psychanalytique de Paris; he talked about a very difficult patient who had led him to develop his conception of the *as if* personality[1] and the way of treating that personality. I think he also talked to us on that day about the capacity to be alone with someone.

*Anne Clancier*:   That seems to me to be one of his most important articles.

*EK*:   It's quite crucial. You know that my present practice is very taken up with psychotics, and I believe that the capacity to be alone with someone is the most operational, the most heuristic concept, one of those that have served me most in understanding patients.

Talking to us about a woman in her fifties, a psychotic, Winnicott showed us how, in the impossibility of doing anything, he had realized that she needed to be silent with him and that when she spoke, she developed an 'as if' personality. That's all I remember of that lecture, but, as you see, it is something of fundamental importance to me. At the time, Winnicott was received with a great deal of reserve. It was said that he was eccentric, that he had an inadequate knowledge of psychoanalysis, and his brilliant clinical intuition was misunderstood. Winnicott began to be quoted only in the last years of his life and at first by child psychoanalysts.

Then I met Winnicott at various conferences. In late 1960, I gave a lecture on the character neuroses to the British Psychoanalytical Society. As almost always Winnicott gave the impression that he was asleep when he was listening, and then he asked me the most pertinent question that one could possibly ask on what I had said and on the point that was certainly the most controversial. Later, I met him at Stockholm in 1963. He had such an unconventional side to him that he sometimes seemed strange, odd: to my great fright, I have seen him cross a street when nobody else would do so and felt sure that he would be run over – he wasn't. I think the drivers saw that he was not looking, for indeed he gave the impression that he was not looking, as if he were moving in a world of his own.

*AC*: Could we say that it was a kind of retreat?

*EK*: Not a pathological retreat, in the sense of withdrawal. I would say that it is a kind of recourse to some inner resources.

*AC*: A word has to be found for it. I was thinking of retreat, in the sense that people go on a retreat.

*EK*: One had the impression that he distanced himself in that way from whatever might distract him. He withdrew into himself with total contempt for the outside world.

*AC*: When, later, he was ill, it was perhaps thanks to that characteristic that he was able to struggle against the disease and emerge once again alive after an attack, in the way that some of my colleagues have described it to me.

*EK*: Yes, probably. I believe that he had auto-erotic capacities of a quite remarkable kind. Paradoxical, no doubt, given social conformism, but certainly without any sense of guilt.

*AC:* His wife, Clare Winnicott, tells how he played all the time. And that when they were together they seemed to be playing.

*EK:* I believe it was thanks to that that he was able to invent the squiggle.

*AC:* Mrs Winnicott describes how he had a cupboard full of squiggles. It was his game.

*EK:* Yes. It was that quite remarkable auto-erotic capacity that also seemed to run throughout his work.

*AC:* What was also remarkable about it was that it was without guilt, whereas many of us hide from it.

*EK:* And I would say without perversion, without perverseness.

*AC:* Without perversion, or shame.

*EK:* Which is very rare.

*AC:* One sometimes meets that with the English, who are capable of being both terribly conformist and very original.

*EK:* Yes, he had that very English side to him.

*AC:* The Lewis Carroll side.

*EK:* Yes, absolutely, without the terrorizing side, it was as if Winnicott had found a sort of grace in living.

*AC:* Which concepts interest you most in Winnicott?

*EK:* I have been interested above all, following Winnicott, yet at the same time keeping my distance, in the transitional object and his conception of the self.

It was by setting out from Winnicott's view, but in a different way, that we described the self.[2] Winnicott was a sort of yeast that enabled us to elaborate a concept that is not the same as his, but which owes it something.

*AC:* After Winnicott's seminars, I gave a seminar on the self and we studied your report to the Congrès des Langues romanes on genetic psychoanalysis. I had the impression that Winnicott had been very important for you.

*EK:* I don't know whether we already referred to Winnicott in our work, but at the time Winnicott was criticized for describing the self on the basis of a false self. It may be that the notion of false self is clearer in his work than that of the self.

I believe that we owe a great deal to Winnicott in the elaboration of ideas on the self. The idea of the transitional object was a sort of yeast for our own elaboration. Of course, it ended up as something different, since we now think that the self is the first psychical configuration that functions within the ego, but with a certain specificity, but which perhaps gives rise not to specific representations but to specific feelings, which are not to be confused with what belongs to the object. The self is, I believe, the element of the object in auto-eroticism, that is to say, in narcissism, but without the object being recognized as distinct. The hallucinatory satisfaction of desire may be the first manifestation of the psychical functioning at the same time as the first manifestation of the self, before the ego is the agency that envelops self and object. Perhaps it is a pre-ego, but one that is not to be confused with the ego that continues to function at the level of auto-eroticism and is more or less bound up with or separated from the object. It is at a deeper level, not necessarily more archaic, but deeper. This is something that Winnicott stresses.

*AC*:   That is interesting. It seems to me that, like Winnicott, you use a paradoxical mode of thought. Saying that it is not what is archaic that is deepest certainly looks like a paradox.

*EK*:   I believe that our clinical work forces that conclusion upon us. If one sees a varied range of patients – neurotics, psychotics, adolescents, children – one is certainly forced to acknowledge that the most archaic is not necessarily the deepest, and vice versa.

I owe a great deal to Winnicott at the level of auto-eroticism. This is something fundamental, which he has laid great stress on. But I believe, unlike him, that the transitional object is already an elaboration, that it is an encounter between the projection of auto-eroticism and the cathection of the object, and therefore already an elaboration of the object and of the self in an encounter. I believe, for example, that schizophrenics have no transitional object.

*AC*:   You have more experience than I in this field, but I would not be surprised if that were the case.

*EK*:   I am quite definite on the matter. Relentless masturbation, for example, has nothing to do with the auto-erotic use of the transitional object.

*AC*  Winnicott says – another paradox – that the transitional object is neither outside nor inside. What do you think?

# Winnicott and Paradox

EK:   It's a notion that I find very sympathetic. I have made a distinction between the organization of the fetishistic relationship, the object as fetish and the transitional object. The transitional object is neither outside nor inside, in the sense that it is based on a thing-object which represents the internal object, but at the same time, one on which the subject projects himself. Therefore it is an object that is not experienced as an external object, since it is a projection of the subject and related to the object. It is different from what I call the fetishistic relationship, since, as we have seen in therapy, for example, the animated object must acquire the quality of being unanimated in order to remain permanent and to be a guarantee of narcissism. The transitional object, on the other hand, is more complex, more subtle, and certainly less archaic, and it has a ludic dimension, a quality of specific pleasure that is absent from the fetishistic relationship. I used Winnicott a great deal, not necessarily to follow in his footsteps but as a yeast to my own thought. I mean that he has always given me a great deal to think about.

AC:   I like your formula, for it seems to correspond perfectly to the impression that I have had in studying Winnicott.

EK:   Yes, he raises lots of things. He raises the question of auto-eroticism and interior play.

AC:   One always gets something out of him. Winnicott makes one invent.

There is another interesting concept, but one that is difficult to define, namely the difference between 'fantasy' and 'fantasying'. It might be said that between fantasy . . . and . . .

EK:   And daydreaming (*rêvasserie*).

AC:   Ah! I was looking for the word. Daydreaming is very good, because it's like a machine ticking over without a load.

EK:   Yes, I think daydreaming is to fantasy what a photograph is to life. Daydreaming is sterile, repetitive. It lacks the dimension of fantasy creation. It's a kind of desiccation of a fantasy into a narrative, shaped, but in a shape that's not very creative. It's like certain literary or musical works. You might say it's like the work of Brücke as compared with that of Beethoven. It's well turned, but a bit boring, a bit desiccated.

Adolescents are very well aware of this because they experience their daydreams as something gloomy and one might almost say tiring. When one has worked a great deal with adolescents, one becomes very aware of the distinction they draw between their daydreams and their 'dreams', in the sense of projects. Having dreams in that sense is something that moves forward, whereas daydreaming is something closed, something that catches you in its toils, something that swirls around you like fog. It's like a grey, drizzly day. Dreaming about the future, on the other hand, may be stormy, but at least there is movement.

*AC:*  Isn't there pleasure in daydreaming, though?

*EK:*  Yes, there is pleasure, but it's a gloomy sort of pleasure, like the pleasure derived from mechanical masturbation, in which the eroticism is repressed and thwarted. Adolescents are well aware of the difference. Thus one sometimes sees them suddenly come to life, there's a light in their eyes, but they need some object or project to reanimate them.

*AC:*  Maybe it's as if they no longer had any contact with an object in the relationship.

*EK:*  They lose it – it's a degraded, rather dehiscent object.

*AC:*  Do you think there is any connection there with anality?

*EK:*  It isn't 'anchored' to it, as you might say, but it may be connected to a certain level of anality. It's a sort of emotional evasion, not putrid, but without smell or savour.

*AC:*  Are you interested in the squiggles?

*EK:*  Yes, they interest me a great deal, but as far as Winnicott's book, *Therapeutic Consultations*, is concerned, I had many reservations and was even very negative in my attitude to it. I think that if one took it as a method, it would be catastrophic. Indeed, you need Winnicott's own genius and creativity to make it work. If one tried to imitate it, it would be transmitted magic, a mere conjuring trick: whereas it must be nourished by all Winnicott's intuitive genius. He had extraordinary capacities and very long, very deep experience behind him.

*AC:*  Do you use Winnicott's books in your teaching?

*EK:*  There was a Winnicott fashion that did no good at all. It was, I believe, a way of not reading Freud. Winnicott, however, knew Freud's work very well – and Melanie Klein's –

and he accommodated them both in his own way. He plundered them to make his own honey. In my teaching I don't often quote authors, because I don't always have the lectures in my head, but I believe I often have Winnicott in my head, whether to agree with him or not.

There was a time when people were using such notions as transitional space quite wrongly. It didn't do Winnicott any good. If one becomes the prisoner of a conceptualization, one goes right against his way of thinking. What is important is that one should work out one's own ideas. Anyway, that is my understanding of Winnicott – it doesn't have to be valid for anyone else.

I'd like to say a word about illusion. A great deal has been said about illusion, in relation to parents and children, but I would like to say something about it in relation to the treatment of psychotics. It is something quite fundamental in that area. If one spends one's time treating psychotics, one has to have a degree of illusion to emerge from repetition, but not too much to enclose the patient in an illusory environment and to reduce their psychical mode of functioning to ours. I use this a great deal in the teaching I do on the psychotherapy of psychotics. One needs enough illusion to believe that one will overcome repetition and alter the psychical economy, and as long as the economy is not altered, one remains in an area in which the translation of contents produces wrong meanings. The patients are enclosed in our understanding, one takes their place, and in fact one is rejecting them. One is not allowing them to develop according to their own rhythm. Winnicott's intuition was to grasp the rhythm of each of the individuals he dealt with, though he didn't put it in these terms. I am putting it in Freud's terms. Freud wrote something quite crucial about rhythm and I find it extremely valuable, both in the direct observation of mother–child relationships and in the case of psychotics. It is the 'counter-time' or counter-rhythm that is most harmful to the child's psychical organizations.

Lastly, there is certainly much more in Winnicott's work than I have derived from it – I've simply been saying a few things about what it has meant to me.

## An inimitable genius
## Interview with Serge Lebovici

*Serge Lebovici*:    I met Winnicott immediately after the war. With
René Diatkine, I took part in a conference organized by the
International Association of Mental Health. It must have been
in 1946. We sat in on Winnicott's consultations at Paddington
Green Hospital. We were very struck by his methods. He
stayed with a family and a child for ten minutes, for example,
then he went to join another family, jumping over the seats.
As we listened to him, it seemed to us that he was clearly a
man inspired. We had been impressed by the quality of
contact that he had with families and children and the great
air of freedom about him. I believe that this freedom can be
most dangerous when Winnicott's zealous followers try to
imitate him.

I then saw Winnicott again during the Annual Days of
Child Psychoanalysis, in 1949, I think, at the Hôpital des
Enfants Malades. Each year we invited a foreign colleague:
later we had Melanie Klein, but Winnicott was the first to be
asked. Now Augusta Bonnard, a pupil of Anna Freud's, a
famous old lady of the time, because she had written an article
on the treatment of a child carried out through the mother,
had also been invited. She had not been told that Winnicott
would also be there. It didn't occur to me to tell her because it
was not a secret. But when she saw him in the room, she cried:
'Oh! There's the murderer.' That gives some idea of how
Winnicott was regarded at the time by Anna Freud's pupils.
I'm not saying that this is how Augusta Bonnard actually
regarded Winnicott, but certainly some of her pupils did.

From then on I remained on very good terms with Winnicott and I would like to talk to you about two occasions that
impressed me. Once, during an International Congress of
Psychoanalysis, he chaired a session. Someone was reading a
paper. I then saw Winnicott put his head down on his hands
on the table, his eyes shut. When the speaker had finished, he
didn't move – I thought he had died. I was horrified. For what
seemed like an interminable time, he didn't move. Then,
suddenly, he sat up as if nothing had happened. Quite

obviously, he hadn't been asleep. I wondered what he was showing by that: interest, a sort of withdrawal into himself? The last time I saw him, I was very moved after the event because I felt that at the time he was drawing away a little from the land of the living: it was at the European Congress of Child Psychology at Wiesbaden. At a conference in Rome I was particularly struck by how much he seemed to be in love with his wife; what she told me did not seem in any way exaggerated, when she spoke of the way he danced with her at conference receptions. And I saw him at the Institut de Psychanalyse, where he was a guest of Sacha Nacht and me, saying how delighted he was to be in Paris, to drink champagne, etc. He was a man who loved life and knew how to live.

On the scientific level, I think Winnicott is a model of the transition from medicine to psychoanalysis, with no intermediary stage in psychiatry. He was initially a paediatrician, then a child psychiatrist, but without really going through psychiatry. He left out the less good part of that discipline. It's not that I am anti-psychiatry, but I think he cut out the least good part of psychiatry by trusting that narrow nosography. With hindsight one sees the extent to which he was a precursor.

For example, what we are now discovering about the life of the infant shows that he had already made some remarkable observations. We didn't believe in them at the time, but what I saw recently (on a videotape during a conference) concerning infants shows how right Winnicott was.

One of the most fascinating parts of his work concerns the mother–infant relationship. The nature of this relationship for Winnicott does not conform to psychoanalytic tradition. His postulate on the set-up of infant and maternal care is the fundamental premise of his theories and his qualities of observation as a paediatrician played a large part in this, as did the type of dazzling intuition that was his.

It has happened to me, too, in therapeutic consultations with children, to feel things as he did, what he calls 'the sacred moments'. It's marvellous, but there is no method in it. Many people work out fixed schemata for all consultations of this type, but they are quite inapplicable if one lacks the capacity to use them.

*Anne Clancier:*   Capacity and long experience.

*SL:*   Yes, one has to be able to identify with every little baby – not everybody can do that. I think he is right when he says that the holding environment is never expressible in analysis. I think one can say the kind of things he says, have intuitions like his, only if one experiences the relationship at a very deep level.

Take, for example, a child having sleep disturbances. Yesterday I saw a video of the first observation I'd done on sleep disturbances. As I was led to see the child again four years later, I looked again at the tape and showed it to my colleagues. I realized that I had said something like Winnicott might had said. The mother had said: 'I never loved anyone as I loved that baby,' but she had not asked that baby to love her. I said to her: 'When you look at him, you don't let him look at you straight in the eyes; he hasn't been able to make a mother of you.' In the end, I think we worked with various interpretations of the catastrophe that had taken place. The whole problem of reconstruction was there: these disasters, which cannot be expressed, which can be expressed only in analysis, must be taken into account and elaborated. Everything Winnicott said on this matter is wonderful. Some people criticize him for these interventions. 'This isn't analysis,' they say. Up to a point, it isn't analysis, but at least he is always an analyst.

Thus in his last, posthumously published book, *The Piggle*, Winnicott recounts how he was sitting next to the two-year-old girl and said to her: 'You're afraid of the greedy Winnicott baby, the baby born out of Piggle and who is very fond of Piggle and wants to eat her.' The little girl then went out to look for her father, sat on his knees and, pointing to the Winnicott baby said, 'I'm shy'; then, 'I'm a baby, too.' She put her head down as if she was emerging head first from between her father's legs. Winnicott then said to her, 'I want to be the only baby'; then, in a different voice, 'Do you have to be angry?' Piggle said 'Yes' and she went on playing, adding, 'I want to be the baby too.' What she did, therefore, was to mime a birth. Winnicott went on playing in front of the father the role of the greedy baby. That is typical of Winnicott's intuition and of his capacity to play not only with the infant, but also in the presence of the father and mother.

AC:   Would you like to say something about other important points in Winnicott's work?

SL:   Yes, I'd like to say a word about holding, about the depressive position, and the self.

The notion of a mother and infant set-up and that of holding seem to me to be impregnable on the level of the theory of development. The union between the child and maternal care is the tool that I am using at present most often to make people who are not analysts feel and understand what psychoanalytic theory is. Thus when I have to deal with problems concerning the child and his mother with first-year students, I talk about Winnicott. The word holding is very telling. When I speak of the mother and the child, of the mother in an almost psychotic state after the child's birth, of the sated and angry child, everything goes very well, that is to say, it makes sense, it's assimilable for people who are fairly attentive.

It's the same in the case of the depressive position.

When we come to the notions of the self and the transitional object, a lot of nonsense is talked. They are notions that don't fit into psychoanalytic theory, are still very phenomenological. I don't see the need to refer to the object relation in that case. But nevertheless it is true that there is an area of culture and idealization, of religion and creativity, where the metaphor of the transitional object extended to creativity makes sense. Nevertheless, in a coherent theory of the object relation, I don't see the need for it, especially as there might be a confusion between it and fetishism.

Another excellent formula is Winnicott's notion that the child must be capable of playing alone in his mother's presence.

As for the self, I think there is something true about it at the developmental level, though it may be a source of confusion, because the word self has different connotations from one country or author to another. But if one defines the self as a continuous experience of maternal care, as Winnicott does, it is an indispensable notion, and I don't think one can understand narcissistic neuroses without reference to it.

The false self often leads to regrettable confusion. Thus the self is confused with 'as if' personalities. It is not the same thing at all. The notion of 'as if' is interesting in clinical work, but the self is a metapsychological notion. Winnicott says that we all to a greater or lesser degree have a false self and that the self cannot be seen.

I find that this reference to what cannot be seen or heard, and will never be seen or heard, may be the most prophetic thing in Winnicott's theories. I think it deserves to be studied much more seriously and has been the victim of a fashion.

I would like to go back to some rather anecdotal details that seem to me to be interesting for those who like Winnicott. For a long time Winnicott found it difficult to get accepted, even in England, yet the last time I was in London for a conference on child psychoanalysis, Anna Freud, who took part in the conference, seemed much more tolerant to Winnicott than she used to be. The fact that he was for a time Dean of the British Psychoanalytical Society certainly went some way to altering his colleagues' attitude.

I've just remembered that the last time I met Winnicott was at the funeral of a British colleague, Joffe; I was representing the International Psychoanalytical Society. Winnicott delivered the funeral oration; it was shortly before his own death.

AC:   I, too, met him shortly before his death. It was at the inauguration of the statue of Freud. He was standing next to me while the speeches were being made: it was very cold and his cheeks and lips were blue. I knew he had a bad heart and I was afraid throughout the ceremony that he might die at any moment. He survived it however.

SL:   Yes, he even got better, because at Joffe's funeral he made an excellent speech in the columbarium – it was very clear and very English in style.

To conclude, I would say that one should not try to imitate Winnicott, as many have done, because it is not enough to apply certain formulas to have his intuition and clinical experience. He himself possessed these qualities to the utmost degree. One might say that Winnicott was an inimitable genius.

## Paradoxes of the Winnicott effect
## Interview with J-B Pontalis

*J-B Pontalis*:    You want to know how I first met Winnicott. The man – with his mobile face, his speech, which was both daring and timid, the hesitant search for the right words, and the failure to find them – I only caught a glimpse of him on two or three occasions. What I did meet – encounter would be a better word, in the sense that it brought about a change in me – was his work. I have to say that a cursory reading of his first works in French translation did not make a strong impression on me: I did not grasp at first what was so original about it. Being neither a paediatrician nor a child analyst, I said to myself rather stupidly that he was not an author for me! It was only later, thanks to contacts that I was able to have with British colleagues, that I came to Winnicott. There were Anglo-French colloquia that brought together, over a week-end, about thirty analysts, young and not so young, of very different theoretical orientations. The exchanges took place, not as we would do in France, around some theoretical or technical problem, but around some very precise 'material': a few sessions or even one session of analysis. The question, which has since become rather commonplace, 'What takes place between a particular analyst and a particular patient?', was posed there in terms of actual experience. During these meetings – which were a sort of 'control' without a 'controller' – I was aware of the fact that our British colleagues always tried to enter and to remain in contact with their patients' – and their own – psychical movements. By psychical movements, I mean, over and above content, text, session, the dynamics of the psyche, the operations of thought that emerge and take place, the subjacent affects, the succession of moods, sometimes of an extremely subtle nature. They also revealed a capacity – which is also rare in our Parisian circles – to subject oneself to others' thought. It seemed to me that

Winnicott had something to do with this quality of exchange. After the violent confrontation between 'Kleinians' and 'Freudians' (as the followers of Anna Freud were called in England), there was formed, as you know, a 'middle group'. Between these irreconcilable adversaries, these Capulets and Montagus of the closed world of analysis, there was needed an open, transitional space, in which paradox could flourish rather than contradictions be allowed to sharpen and become frozen. Winnicott never wanted to be the leader of this intermediate group: he had never offered himself as a Master. That, too, pleased me enormously.

So it was the atmosphere of those meetings – an atmosphere that, looking back, I may tend to idealize – that led me to read Winnicott more attentively. To this was added a friendly influence, that of Masud Khan, whose vigorous non-dogmatism and clinical insight I have always admired. In fact, I don't think I have really 'worked' on Winnicott's books. I would say rather that I have 'consulted' them in the sense that he gave to 'therapeutic consultation': a few pages have often got me out of a corner in difficult cases.

It was during this period that I published some articles by Winnicott in the *Nouvelle Revue de psychanalyse*, notably 'Fear of Breakdown', and translated, with Claude Monod, *Playing and Reality*.

AC:  What now strikes you as the most interesting of Winnicott's concepts?

J-BP:  It's not so much the concepts that interest me in him and I imagine he would share this way of looking at things! Anybody can produce concepts – Winnicott's genius does not lie in that direction.

For example, I was and remain reticent about the use of the 'concept' of the transitional object, which is now applied quite wrongly. On the other hand, without in fact being able to assess precisely the extent of my debt, I have used the intuition that underlies that concept, an intuition that no doubt justified for Winnicott the importance that he gave to the object and above all to the transitional *phenomena*. What I have written on the object-dream, on the gap, even antinomy, between the production of dreams and the capacity to dream, comes more or less directly from Winnicott. And, in a more general way, the notion that mental activity was really significant for the subject only if it was not purely mental, simply a matter of mechanical representations, but became embodied in the psychical life.

A great psychoanalyst, for someone who has not had the luck to work with him, can be recognized by this: whenever one reads him, it's a good session! An inhibition in thought is lifted, a bit of psychical space comes alive. Winnicott did not provide a theoretical grid, as Melanie Klein did. One might say that there are 'Kleinian' patients. I don't think there are 'Winnicottian' ones.

*AC*: Yes, it is rather in the interventions one makes that one feels oneself to be Winnicottian, without setting out to.

*J-BP*: Your remark reminds me of a moment in analysis. The patient was apparently playing the game of free association, perhaps rather too methodically, but he was never short of dreams and ideas and I never short of interpretations! We were, I think, at the limits of what Winnicott calls the 'psychoanalytical' game, in which everyone benefits except the analysis! So this model analysand – this model child – brought me a lot of dreams, which he tried to decipher and get me to decipher, supposing me, quite wrongly, to be more expert than he in the art of deciphering. During a session, we were interrupted by several telephone calls that I had to take. For a time, I didn't feel very aware of this patient, I felt aware rather of his absence from himself, I felt in communication, if I may put it like this, with what was absent rather than with what he was saying. In fact, for me, he was like one of those people who ring you from a long way off, and you can't hear a word they're saying except a repeated 'Please hold the line'. And there was this man, usually so docile, for once making a request, in what was certainly a moderate, but for him quite firm way. Without raising his voice, he said: 'You ought to have an answering machine.' And, probably because at the time I was unknown to myself under the influence of Winnicott I replied immediately: 'No doubt that's what you want; you'd like me to be an answering machine, but that's certainly not what you need.' I felt, without really being aware of it, that this patient wanted me to be an interpreting machine as he, for want of anything better, was a machine for dreaming, associating, elaborating. But what he lacked was the ability to recognize that he needed someone, someone who would be there for him alone. And he didn't feel that he had a right to ask that, certain that he would not get an answer. No answer *in himself*.

AC:    It was probably the first time he showed you that he had any need . . .

J-BP:    Yes, it was the first time that something hidden was manifested, for both of us. For my own spontaneous intervention had disconcerted me as much as him. After the event it made me perceive positively in him what, for some time, I had been formulating in negative terms, at a distance: he intellectualized too much, so he felt nothing, etc. That day, this patient became for me something else, another *person*, close to me, instead of a distant *fellow creature*. I knew that he had lost his parents as a child. I knew it, but, like him, I could only state it as a fact. Only state the poverty of the memories of his early years. Only state what had come in their place: an active cathexis and an incessant flow of words. From that session on, we were able to bring the mother into the analysis. The good-enough mother, not the good or bad mother, but, the one who is enough, the one who is enough that, at the right moment, one can do without her. But to do without her, she has to be there first: again a paradox!

AC:    It's moments like that that teach us a lot of things about our patients, about ourselves, and enable us to grasp what is at stake in analytical treatment.

J-BP:    I'd like to come back to Winnicott's concept, to one of them in particular, that of the 'use of the object'. I would say that Winnicott allows himself to be used. Take, for example, the notion of the 'false self'. I have criticized it myself: theoretically, it seems to me unacceptable, especially when it is substantified, treated as an agency (*instance*) or as a noso-graphical entity. Nevertheless it corresponds to an unquestionable clinical intuition. The idea that certain subjects must construct a borrowed edifice for themselves in order to protect or to conceal their 'hidden self' – as Masud Khan would say –

*Winnicott and Paradox*

which is itself too fragile and threatened, such an idea has not only a descriptive, but an operational value. In France, we are fond of forging 'neoconcepts', if only to separate ourselves off from our masters and colleagues. After all one applies them, one always finds something to justify their relevance. Winnicott proceeds in the reverse direction: he finds something – difficult cases that have forced him to find it and, as best he can – because he is not a Freudologist – he puts words on to his discovery. You sense this in his writings: a lot of banalities and then, suddenly, the illumination, the dazzling breakthrough occurs in a sentence.

*AC*:   You are one of the few psychoanalysts, among those who I have interviewed, who have literary activities, as much in the area of creation as in that of criticism. Has Winnicott meant anything to you in that respect?

*J-BP*:   There is a text of his that, a long time ago, impressed me greatly. It's a very short text, called, again paradoxically, 'Communicating and Not Communicating'. In it Winnicott speaks, if I remember rightly, of the adolescent and his double, contradictory desire to communicate and not to communicate. He also refers in it to the writer and, I think, particularly to Henry James, whose art, which is as captivating as it is irritating, is to move around a secret, which may, in fact, be nothing at all. There is an analogy here, a fairly obvious closeness between psychoanalysis and literature. In it we see at work, through quite different ways of course (literature lives by disguise, it is, after all, less a matter of 'lying' than is analysis), the same postulate: to be, for the first time, heard, recognized, even in what one is oneself unaware of, and in the same movement, to fear being absorbed by someone else's thought and language.

An area of illusion, going beyond the divisions between me and not-me, inside and outside, might also be a good definition of the writer and reader. Through the analysis of the patient, the analyst is altered. From a book that one has written or read, one emerges different from the person one thought one was.

*AC*:   What do you think of the notion of creativity as understood by Winnicott?

*J-BP*:   I don't care for the word, still less for its promotion, here, there and everywhere. Trying to get everybody to believe that there is a treasure inside him is a false scent. To say, as Winnicott does, even with humour, that one can be as creative in frying eggs as Schumann composing a sonata, don't you find that rather excessive? If I express an emotion, that does not mean that I am creative. I'm afraid that Winnicott there was taken in to some extent by his love for children (and for mothers). Having said this – and here, again, I reject the concept, but recognize the thing – when Winnicott speaks of creativity, he reminds us that the world of our perceptions is a dead letter as long as it is not animated by a look. In this sense, we create the world . . . But it is already there. Creating *a* world is another matter, however. There it is a question of bringing to birth the new in a given culture. Winnicott succeeded in giving this in the psychoanalytical 'culture' no doubt because he came from elsewhere, because he was not made to measure for it. A personal tradition helps one to be original, not of the system.

One can trace back Freud's thought, one can expound Melanie Klein's theory, one can systematize Lacan's theories even more. If you try to do that with Winnicott, you lose what is best in him. What I have been and remain sensitive to is the Winnicott effect.

## Freedom of thought
## Interview with Daniel Widlöcher

*Daniel Widlöcher*:   I first knew Winnicott through his article on intermediate space, which had been translated and published in the *Revue française de psychanalyse*; later, I got to know his work better. Two of his contributions interested me particularly. First, his work on the general theory of development, on the relationship between the mother and the child, on the facilitating environment. The *International Journal of Psychoanalysis* asked me to write an article on Winnicott's book, *The Maturational Processes and the Facilitating Environment*. I wrote an enthusiastic review, while criticizing certain aspects of Winnicott's work. Winnicott replied to me and showed interest in the analysis that I had done.

The second pole of interest was for me the squiggle game, for I had been very struck by what Winnicott proposed. Since I was myself working a great deal on children's drawing, I was often scandalized by the way psychoanalytic interpretations were imposed on drawings that were highly constructed, very elaborated, very secondary, in the sense of secondary processes, and on which hypotheses and interpretations were built rather as on tea leaves at the bottom of a cup. What I admired a great deal in Winnicott was the way in which he induced an atmosphere of formal regression, of fantasy activity in the child – that is to say, the activity of scribbling, the child's graffiti, was not a production, but a gesture almost like a dream, in which the child's imagination was given full rein. I found that very positive in counterbalancing a sort of rigidity with which drawings were treated by the French, as a document to be deciphered, rather like a dream text.

At that time, I had the good fortune to meet Winnicott at a conference. He was then invited to France by a colleague, Granoff, who ran a children's centre at Nanterre. Winnicott had been asked to communicate with families and children, through the squiggle game, and I invited him to take part in this group. Winnicott was impressed at the idea of doing drawings for French children, Parisian children, while he claimed that he did not speak French at all, which was not quite true, but he was so worried that he asked someone in the room to act as interpreter. This was how I had the privilege of attending a squiggle game with Winnicott.

A small boy was waiting in the waiting room, without being in any way prepared for this contact, and he suddenly found himself sitting next to this old Englishman who purred and miaowed like a cat, in order to make contact with the child almost without using French. I translated nothing, I was there in case there might be some problem to be resolved, I was quite passive, quite outside the relationship. It is obvious that the contact that was made, the child's delight, the closeness of the child to this man who did not speak his language and who was supposed not to understand it, the way in which the child formulated things concerning his fantasy life, his memories, in so short a time and in such astonishing intimacy, obviously convinced me of what I had first read in the books and articles. For me it was a most instructive encounter, one that later led me to develop – I won't go as far as to say the squiggle game – but any contact with a child that makes him begin to dream with the adult and not to remain frozen in a rigid attitude, as one sees so often in consultations, even in psychotherapy. That for me really was a turning-point in my life.

*Anne Clancier:* I had the same impression when, in London, I saw Winnicott practise the squiggle game, but it struck me as even more extraordinary that he was able to do it with a child who didn't speak the same language.

*DW:* Yes, he was with a little fellow who had an extraordinary Parisian accent and who was no doubt wondering what he was doing there with this white-haired Englishman.

*AC:* Your phrase 'the child starts to dream with the adult' seems an excellent one to me and highly significant of what could take place with Winnicott.

*DW:* Before, I was a bit reticent about Winnicott's theories. It seemed to me that their clinical richness was not always linked to theoretical rigour; in particular the concept of intermediate or transitional space bothered me rather by its empirical, very intuitive aspect.

Later, I was bothered, too, by Winnicott's success, by the reception accorded to any article he happened to publish at the time, by a Winnicott fashion that was then spreading. Nevertheless, I believe that it did have the merit of providing a sort of justification of emotion, the affect, the affective participation in the therapist's relationship with his patient. In short, it counterbalanced a rather intellectualist formalism that was particularly common at the time. Winnicott served as an antidote. He was certainly one of the best agents of the influence of the British school on French psychoanalysis, not only in terms of psychoanalytical theory, but also on French psychoanalytical practice. Winnicott brought a great deal, especially to young psychoanalysts, by making them aware of the dimensions that a rather cold or academic theory would not enable them to perceive.

Although subsequently I have distanced myself to some extent from Winnicott's positions, I do share with him that concern to take into account in treatment mobilizing emotional charges and the need to induce an atmosphere of regression. Indeed I insisted in my report to the Barcelona Conference on the value of a communication that is not only a communication of information.

It cannot be said that Winnicott provides an original overall theory in relation to psychoanalytical theory and indeed I cannot see why he should do so – and he certainly never made such a claim. I simply mistrusted a certain enthusiasm for Winnicott that struck me sometimes as rather disturbing.

*AC*: Perhaps one might situate Winnicott in relation to Melanie Klein. It seems to me that Klein is more of a theoretician, whereas Winnicott provides the raw material, interesting, even valuable as it is, but leaves us to erect the building. So Melanie Klein and Winnicott respond better to analysts of different temperaments, but Winnicott is particularly appreciated by those who are fond above all of clinical practice and who lay particular stress on intuition.

*DW*: I agree and I would say that certain Kleinians in Europe and in England have a fairly rigid theory, whereas in France they seem to be much more subtle.

At the risk of generalizing too much, I would say that there are two categories of psychoanalytic works, those that provide theories, metapsychological concepts in the formalized, that is to say, highly rational language of science, and those that contribute what might be called, depending on the case, psychoanalytic poetry or psychoanalytic fiction. What I am saying here is not at all intended to be pejorative: I just want to stress that there are works that offer the reader not so much a knowledge of theory and hypothesis as an aid to thinking analytically while reading the book.

*WC*: One might say that this allows the functioning of imaginative thought.

*DW*: Yes, for example, I have had people on the couch saying things like: 'I admire Winnicott, because when I read him I feel a bit more like a psychoanalyst.' You may regard that as good or bad; good because it may help certain patients to

146

develop their capacity for thought, their psychoanalytic mind, but bad because people who have great difficulties in being analysts, when they are unable to find pleasure in their analytical thinking when it is tied up with their practice, sometimes compensate for that by their reading. What is left to them is only fiction . . . that is why I spoke of psycho-analytic fiction.

AC: It might be said that, in France, there were two opposite tendencies at a certain time. There were the psychoanalysts who needed to cling to language, to a sort of formalism, and who found their support in the work of Lacan, and those who, on the contrary, gave precedence to the thera-peutic relationship, the affect, and therefore to Winnicott's works.

DW: Yes, that was also my impression at a certain time.

AC: You spoke of your interest in the squiggle game. It always seemed to me when I watched Winnicott that there was a sort of creation when he practised this game with a child. Don't you think there was something of the artist in Winnicott? You have worked a great deal on art and written about children's drawing, on painting, especially on the work of the painter Segantini, don't you think that to analyse art in a productive way one has to be something of a Winnicottian?

DW: Yes, Winnicott was much more interested in the creative act and in the mental operations that made it possible than in the meaning of the thing created, as psychoanalysts had previously been. Winnicott has enabled others after him to transpose into other areas what he felt to be very important in the analytical situation. The risk is that some people have been able to interpret Winnicott's works as an authorization of a kind of spontaneism, whereas in him there was a very profound knowledge of psychoanalytic technique and practice.

AC: Yes, I have often heard, in seminars, Winnicott's words quoted by people who wanted to criticize him. Torn out of context and distorted, they lost the meaning that they had in Winnicott's work. So one must always keep very close to his text if one is to avoid misunderstanding what he meant or what he was trying to do in his analyses.

What other aspects of Winnicott's work have been of particular interest to you?

DW:   On the question of transitional space, which we mentioned earlier, I am no longer entirely in agreement with this concept. I believe much more in the creation of a common space between two people who begin to function on the same level and in the same register, and who create a common dream space, rather than relating that to the concept of an object that is not quite the 'me', but which is not yet the 'not-me' either. It may be useful to represent a particular moment in the child's development and to find some trace of it in the adult, but I don't believe that it is necessary to make it the foundation of interpersonal relationships. I think that would be excessive.

On the other hand, I have found the concept of the false self extremely important, particularly in understanding certain mechanisms in infantile psychosis. There clinical experience completely confirms Winnicott's hypothesis. An excessive use has been made of the false self and nowadays one finds people calling any defensive armature the false self. I don't think Winnicott can be blamed for this excessive use, for from what I know of his text on the false self his use of the concept seems very precise; the term refers to a particular mode of response to dissociation but does not seem to me to justify generalizations.

AC:   Winnicott said that we all have a certain false self within us. Perhaps it's what others have called the social ego.

DW:   Yes, we all have aspects that are not very linked to our libidinal dynamics and which nevertheless function. Winnicott's concepts being both intuitive and very concrete, and not very articulated theoretically, it is easier to reduce them to some banal use than others: it's the risk one runs with Winnicott.

AC:   Has Winnicott's work had any consequences as far as your clinical practice is concerned?

DW:   Winnicott certainly helped me to internalize a greater freedom of action and thought with children. I haven't practised child psychotherapy for some years, but in the early 1960s this led me to a very different kind of practice with children. With adults, Winnicott's influence may have led me, not in the direction of a freedom of action, but of a freedom of thought. By that I mean that I allowed myself in a way a certain emotional warmth and a recognition that this was something fundamental. What Winnicott has to say about holding in the analytical situation – which does not mean attitudes of support or reassurance – is fundamental. Too often, I think, people have confused an emotional atmosphere with directive interventions.

It should be said that, as a psychoanalyst, Winnicott did have interventions of this type, but he was dealing with serious cases, borderline cases, for which it was absolutely necessary to have technical innovations, and a great freedom of approach. That has been very important, because at a time when analysts began to treat serious, fairly atypical cases, Winnicott was beginning to work out a theorization adapted to these problems.

I have the impression that I use Winnicott less now, but I don't at all think that this relates to any decline in Winnicott's work.

*AC:*  After a temporary fashion, Winnicott will assume his true place.

A lot is talked now about Bion. How do you situate Bion in relation to Winnicott?

*DW:*  Bion is almost the opposite of Winnicott. There is in him a certain hyperformalism in the return to neologism that is sometimes very off-putting, because one has to absorb a lot of definitions before one can come to grips with his thought. However, there is also a fairly poetic style in Bion. At present I am fairly influenced by Bion, because it seems that one needs a sort of general conceptualization of the analytical situation, for example of the notion of the analyst's thought as being directly influenced by the analysand's thought. From this point of view, Bion's ideas are parallel with those of Winnicott. However, they come from very different horizons, since Bion began with group studies, whereas Winnicott doesn't seem to have any interest in groups. He was even rather contemptuous of group techniques.

I would also draw a parallel between Winnicott and Balint,

because they had similar situations. On the historical level of psychoanalytical thought, they were for a time the two great thinkers of the British 'middle group'.

*AC:*   It is worth noting that they both had a psychiatric training; Balint was in general practice as a physician and Winnicott a paediatrician. That probably played a role.

Has your position on children's drawing altered?

*DW:*   No, it is still the same, but I find Winnicott's ideas comforting: the squiggle game, the comparison between the act of graphic elaboration and the dream, regression, I find all that very sympathetic.

To conclude, I would like to stress once again the freedom of thought that Winnicott helps one to acquire.

# Chronology

1896    Birth of Donald Woods Winnicott in Devon, into an English Protestant family. He has two older sisters. At 13, he is sent to the Leys School, Cambridge. At 16, a fracture of the collar-bone confirms him in his wish to become a doctor. He takes a degree in biology at Jesus College, Cambridge. War breaks out and, as a medical student at the university, now turned into a hospital, he works as assistant nurse in 1916. He joins the navy; he is transferred to a destroyer as student surgeon.

        After the war, he continues his medical studies at St Bartholomew's Hospital, London. During his studies, he is hospitalized for three months for an abscess on the lung. Being particularly interested in work with children, he becomes, after passing his exams, a hospital consultant.

1923    Begins psychoanalysis with John Strachey. He is appointed to two hospital posts: one at Queen's Hospital for Children, the other, which he occupied for forty years, at Paddington Green Children's Hospital.

1924    Marries. He opens a practice in Harley Street.

1931    Publication of *Clinical Notes on Disorders of Childhood*, one of the first books, in the field of paediatrics, to link medical treatment and psychiatry.

World War II breaks out and the evacuation of children as a result of the bombing of London leads him to study, among other things, the anti-social tendency and its relations with 'deprivation'.

He continues his work as consultant at Paddington Green as paediatrician and psychoanalyst.

**1951**   'Transitional Objects and Transitional Phenomena', paper read to the British Psychoanalytical Society. The second version was to appear twenty years later in *Playing and Reality*.

Married for the second time, to Clare Brittow.

Appointed a Fellow of the Royal College of Physicians (1944). A Fellow of the British Psychological Society. He is to become President of the Medicine Section and later president of the Paediatrics Section. Twice President of the British Psychoanalytical Society (1956–59 and 1965–68), he was for twenty-five years a teaching member of The Institute of Psycho-Analysis.

**1968**   He is awarded the James Spence Medal for Paediatrics.

**1971**   He dies in London, 25 January, 1971.

# Bibliographical note

Titles of books by Winnicott cited in notes under date of publication.

1957    *The Child and the Family*, London, Tavistock
1965    *The Maturational Processes and the Facilitating Environ-ment*, London, The Hogarth Press and the Institute of Psycho-Analysis
1971a   *Playing and Reality*, London, Tavistock
1971b   *Therapeutic Consultations in Child Psychiatry*, London, The Hogarth Press and the Institute of Psycho-Analysis
1975    *Through Paediatrics to Psychoanalysis*, London, The Hogarth Press and the Institute of Psycho-Analysis
1978    *The Piggle: An Account of the Psychoanalytic Treatment of a Little Girl*, London, The Hogarth Press and the Institute of Psycho-Analysis
1986    *Holding and Interpretation: Fragment of an Analysis*, London, The Hogarth Press and the Institute of Psycho-Analysis

# Notes

## Preface

1. 'The Theory of the Parent–Infant Relationship' (1960), Winnicott (1965: 37–55).
2. Winnicott (1975: 194–203).
3. Winnicott (1971: 26–37).

## Donald Woods Winnicott

1. Clare Winnicott, 'D. W. W.: A Reflection', in Simon A. Grolnick *et al.* (eds). *Between Reality and Fantasy*, London and New York: Jason Aronson, 1978.

## Chapter 1

1. Winnicott (1975: 145).
2. Winnicott (1975: 99).
3. Ibid.
4. Ibid.
5. Freud, Standard Edition, vol. XII, p. 220.
6. 'The Theory of the Parent–Infant Relationship' (Winnicott 1965).
7. Winnicott (1957: 14–15).
8. Ibid., p. 20.
9. Winnicott (1965: 44).

10. Ibid., p. 45.
11. Winnicott (1957: 56).
12. Ibid.
13. Ibid., p. 58.
14. Winnicott (1965: 60). M. A. Sechehaye (1947), *La réalisation symbolique. Nouvelle méthode de psychothérapie appliquée à un cas de schizophrénie*, Berne: Hans Huber; Paris: PUF.
15. E. Glover, *On the Early Development of Mind*, London: Imago, 1932.
16. 'Psychoses and Child Care' (Winnicott 1975: 226).
17. Marion Milner, *The Hands of the Living God*, London: Hogarth/Institute of Psycho-Analysis, 1969.
18. Title of an article in Winnicott, (1975: 204–18). The quotations in this section come from that article.
19. P. Marty and M. Fain, 'Importance du rôle de la motricité dans la relation d'objet'. XVIIe Conférence des Psychanalystes de Langues romanes, Paris, 1954. *Revue française de Psychanalyse*, 1955, 19 (1–2): 205–84.
20. Anna Freud, *The Ego and the Mechanisms of Defence*, London: Hogarth/IP-A, 1937.
21. In this area Winnicott shows that he is in agreement with the ideas of Freud and Melanie Klein as to the need for frustration ('the object is born in hate,' Freud wrote) and its gradual dosage depending on the infant's age, but he greatly developed these ideas through his clinical experience of infants and, in this, turned out to be a precursor of contemporary psychoanalysts, who, for research purposes, carry out observations of infants in the family and in the crèche.
22. Winnicott (1975: 262–77).
23. Charles Rycroft, *A Critical Dictionary of Psychoanalysis*, London: Penguin, 1968, p. 122.
24. Winnicott (1975: 262–72).
25. Rycroft, op. cit., p. 32.
26. Addressing mothers in his 1949 broadcast, 'Weaning', (Winnicott 1957: 64–8).
27. 'The Depressive Position in Normal Emotional Development' (Winnicott 1975: 262–77). The quotations in this section come from this article.
28. Cf. 'Psycho-Analysis and the Sense of Guilt', in John D. Sutherland (ed.), *Psychoanalysis and Contemporary Thought*, London: Hogarth/IP-A, 1958. Winnicott distinguishes between two types of anti-social behaviour. In the first type, 'one tries unconsciously to give meaning to the sense of guilt. . . . It is not so much guilt which is repressed as the fantasy that explains the guilt.' In the other type, it is 'the capacity to feel guilt which is lost' (see later 'The Anti-social Tendency').
29. Melanie Klein, *Psycho-Analysis of Children*, London: Hogarth, 1935.
30. Rycroft, op. cit., p. 86.
31. 'The Manic Defence' (Winnicott 1975: 129–44). All quotations in this section are from this article.

32. Cf. his paper 'Repli et régression', XVIIIe Congrès des Psychanalystes de Langues romanes, Paris, November 1954.
33. Winnicott (1965: 29–36). All quotations in this section are taken from this article.
34. Anne Clancier, 'L'ennui', lecture delivered to the Société Psychanalytique de Paris, 1972.
35. P. Mâle, *Etude psychanalytique de l'adolescence*, Paris: PUF, 1956.


# Chapter 2

1. 'Psychoses and Child Care' (Winnicott 1975: 219–28). Unless otherwise stated quotations in this section are taken from this article.
2. E. Bick, 'The Experience of the Skin in Early Object-relations', *International Journal of Psycho-Analysis*, 1968, 49: 484.
3. D. Anzieu, 'Le moi-peau', *Nouvelle Revue de Psychanalyse*, 1974, 9, Le Dehors et le Dedans: 195–208.
4. 'Dependence in Infant Care, in Child Care, and in the Psycho-Analytic Setting' (1963) (Winnicott 1965: 256).
5. Unless otherwise stated the quotations from this section are from 'Primitive Emotional Development' (Winnicott 1975).
6. 'Basis for Self in Body', *International Journal of Child Psychotherapy*, 1: 1.
7. Ibid.
8. The knowledge of a true 'not-me' also emerges from the intellect and depends on the degree of elaboration and maturity attained by the individual.
9. During treatment, it is necessary to attain a sense of guilt in one's relations with the drives and ideas of aggressiveness and destruction in order to allow the patient to allow this feeling and to assume it. A need for reparation then appears. According to Winnicott, it may take the form of a 'false reparation', connected with the patient's identification with his mother. The dominant feature is not the patient's guilt, but the mother's organized defence against her unconscious depression and guilt. Winnicott believes that the child uses this depression in order to escape his own, thus operating a false reparation and restoration that compromise the development of his own capacity for restitution. Many unexpected scholastic failures, depressions, or false successes on the part of adolescents result from this. ('Reparation in Respect of Mothers' Organized Defence Against Depression', Winnicott 1975: 91–6.)
10. Winnicott (1975: 12–69). All quotations from this section are taken from this article.
11. Freud's observation of the child with the cotton-reel ('Beyond the Pleasure Principle', Standard Edition, vol. XVIII).
12. During a seminar at the Institut E. Claparède (Neuilly-sur-Seine).
13. Winnicott informs us that two weeks later the child no longer had asthma, but the mother, on the other hand, who had suffered asthma

attacks while pregnant with Margaret, had a recurrence of attacks. It
should be noted that her own mother had also begun to have attacks at
the time of her first pregnancy.

14. 'Paediatrics and Psychiatry' (Winnicott 1975: 157–73).
15. Winnicott (1975: 145–56). The remaining quotations in this section are
    from this article.
16. 'Psychoses and Child Care' (Winnicott 1975: 219–28). The quotations in
    this section are taken from this article.
17. Winnicott (1971b). Winnicott cites the case of a breast-fed infant who,
    according to his parents, put up violent resistance to weaning.
18. Cf. S. Freud, 'Mourning and Melancholia', *Collected Papers*, vol. IV,
    London: Hogarth; K. Abraham (1924), Complete Works, vol. II (1913–
    1915), *Development of the Libido. Character Formation*; J. Rickman, 'The
    Development of The Psycho-Analytical Theory of the Psychoses',
    *International Journal of Psycho-Analysis*, 1928, supplement no. 2; M. Klein
    (1934), 'Mourning and Its Relation to Manic Depressive States', *Con-
    tributions to Psycho-Analysis, 1921–1945*, London: Hogarth, 1940.
19. Presented in Prof. J.-M. Alby's seminar on identity, Paris, M.-A.
    Ploix-Bocherau, Mémoire pour le C.E.S. de Psychiatrie, *Mise à l'épreuve
    du groupe dans la formation d'une pédo-psychiatre*, Université de Paris VI,
    Faculté de Médecine Saint-Antoine, 1977.
20. D. Burlingham and A. Freud, *Young Children in Wartime: A Years' Work
    in a Residential War Nursery*, London: Allen & Unwin, 1942; J. Bowlby,
    'A Two-Year-Old Goes to the Hospital', in Bowlby *et al.*, *Psycho-Analytic
    Study of the Child*, vol. VII, New York: International University Press,
    1952; R. Spitz, 'Relevancy of Direct Infant Observation', *Psycho-Analytic
    Study of The Child*, vol. V, New York: International University Press,
    1952.
21. Winnicott suggests that one should see in this the origin of the capacity
    for ambivalence, the term used in ordinary language, when it implies
    that repressed hate has distorted the positive elements in a rela-
    tionship. But, he stresses that this way of putting it should not stop us
    regarding the capacity for ambivalence as a stage in emotional develop-
    ment. Cf. D. Braunschweig and M. Fain, *Eros et Antéros*, Paris: Payot,
    1971.
22. Winnicott (1975: 229–42). The following quotations in this section come
    from this article.
23. In *Holding and Interpretation*, one sees a patient entangled in his capacity
    for reparation, which he feels as a threat, for, for him, satisfaction
    annihilates the object, removes the loss of desire for the breast. In this
    patient 'the intellectualization that isolated his subjective self from
    others and from his own awareness of himself was manifested in a
    perpetual cackle – his fantasying'. This same patient had been the
    subject of an earlier paper ('Withdrawal and Regression', Winnicott
    1975: 255–61), in which Winnicott had referred to the 'medium' ('like
    the oil in which wheels move', as the patient had said). He noticed that
    in this way he had converted withdrawal into regression.

It should be noticed that the 'medium' is the reference that is not to be found in Freud.

## Chapter 3

1. *International Review of Psycho-Analysis*, 1974, 1: 103–07.
2. Ibid.
3. 'Primary Maternal Preoccupation' (1956) (Winnicott 1975: 300–05. The quotations in this section are from that article.
4. It would seem that, according to Winnicott, the development of the ego is characterized by various trends:

    1. The main trend in the maturational process can be gathered into the various meanings of the word *integration*. Integration in time becomes added to (what might be called) integration in space.
    2. The ego is based on a body ego, but it is only when all goes well that the person of the baby starts to be linked with the body and the body-functions, with the skin as the limiting membrane. 'I have used the term *personalization*', says Winnicott, 'to describe this process, because the term depersonalization seems at basis to mean a loss of firm union between ego and body, including id-drives and id-satisfactions. (The term depersonalization has gathered to itself a more sophisticated meaning in psychiatric writings.)'
    3. The ego initiates object-relating.

    'It would seem to be possible to match the three phenomena of ego-growth with three aspects of infant and child-care:

    1. Integration matches with holding.
    2. Personalization matches with handling.
    3. Object-relating matches with object-presenting. ('Ego Integration in Child Development' [1962], Winnicott 1965: 56–63.)

5. 'Fear of Breakdown.' The remaining quotations in this chapter are from this article.
6. Cf. R. Gaddini, 'Bion's Catastrophic Change and Winnicott's Breakdown', *Revista di Psicoanalisi*, Rome 1981: 3–4.
7. We should note the role that Winnicott gives to the pre-natal phase and to the experience of birth. Cf. cases of false self in which the patient achieves the regression that she still needed after a 'classical analysis' ('Mind and Its Relation to the Psyche-Soma', Winnicott 1975: 243–54; 'Metapsychological and Clinical Aspects of Regression within the Psycho-Analytical Set-Up', Winnicott 1975: 278–94).
8. A clinical example of the fear of breakdown was the subject of a paper given by Mrs Winnicott: Clare Winnicott, 'Fear of Breakdown: A Clinical Example', paper read to the 31st International Congress of

Psychoanalysis, New York, August 1979. *International Journal of Psycho-Analysis*, 1980, 61: 351–57.
9. Cf. Georges Amado, who is very close to Winnicott in certain aspects of his thinking. It should be remembered that Winnicott did not accept the death instinct. (G. Amado, *De l'enfant à l'adulte. La Psychanalyse au regard de l'être*, Paris: PUF, 1979.)

# Chapter 4

1. Other words by British authors emerging out of these circumstances were published around the Hampstead Clinic (for example, D. Burlingham and A. Freud, *Infants without Families*, London: Allen & Unwin, 1944, or the Tavistock Clinic (the report by J. Bowlby, 'Psychoanalysis of Child Care', in J. Sutherland (ed.), *Psycho-Analysis and Contemporary Thought*, London: Hogarth, 1958).
2. The title of an article (1956) (Winnicott 1975: 306–15).
3. 'Delinquency as a Sign of Hope', in S. Feinstein and P. L. Giovacchini (ed.), *Adolescent Psychiatry*, vol. II, New York: Basic Books, 1973, pp. 364–71.
4. Winnicott (1971b: 216–19), from which the quotations in this section have been taken.
5. We find here an example of Winnicott's attitude to parents: Can the mother do anything other than 'her best'? Many of the clinical cases published by them show the place that he gives to parents in the therapy of their children when there is an 'environmental failure'.
6. 'Communicating and Not Communicating Leading to a Study of Certain Opposites' (1963) (Winnicott 1965: 179–92).
7. 'Ego Integration in Child Development' (1962) (Winnicott 1965: 56–63).
8. Winnicott (1975: 243–54).
9. Ibid.
10. Winnicott (1965: 140–52).
11. Winnicott recognizes the relationship that exists with Sechehaye's 'symbolic realization', but modifies it slightly: it is the *gesture or hallucination* that are made real, the infant's capacity *to use a symbol* being the consequence of it.
12. 'A surprising assertion,' writes G. Amado. 'We are in the habit of thinking that it is because he does not feel all the imperfections that the infant does not suffer too much at the beginning of life, helped in this by the mother's vigilance and "excitement-conducting" function.' And he notes: 'It is also thought that progress towards autonomy results from the first defence mechanisms and not from precocious independence and the need to "find oneself" in solitude'. (G. Amado, *De l'Enfant à l'adulte. La psychanalyse au regard de l'être*, Paris: PUF, 1979.)
13. One might compare these reflections with Michael Balint's 'three areas of the mind' and 'fundamental flaw' and W. Fairbairn's 'concept of a

central ego'. (M. Balint, *The Fundamental Flaw. Therapeutic Aspects of Regression*, London: Tavistock, 1968; and W. R. D. Fairbairn, *An Object Relation Theory of the Personality*, New York: Basic Books, 1952.)

14. 'Psychoses and Child Care' (1952) (Winnicott 1975: 219–28).
15. This acquisition will be encouraged by the recognition of what is unconscious and conscious in human nature. This is what Winnicott tries to elucidate in 'On Influencing and Being Influenced' and he writes: 'The prostitution of education lies in the bad use of what might almost be called the most sacred quality of the child: *doubts about the self*. The dictator knows this very well and exercises his power by offering a life in which doubt has no place – but how gloomy it is!' (*The Child and the Outside World*.)
16. Winnicott (1986: 19–20). Cf. 'Clinical Varieties of Transference' (Winnicott 1975: 295–99, an article in which Winnicott, on the basis of primary identification, throws light on the analyst's work with such patients.

## Chapter 5

1. Based on a paper given by Jeannine Kalmanovitch at the Institut Claparède (Dr S. Decobert's seminar), 27 April, 1983.
2. Winnicott (1978: 162–63).
3. Was he not to go as far as to say to one patient: 'It is *I* who see the girl and hear a girl talking, when actually there is a man on my couch. The mad person is *myself*' (Winnicott 1971a: 74). Cf. Reik, cited in J.-M. Alby, *Théodore Reik: le trajet d'un psychanalyste de Vienne fin-de-siècle au Nouveau monde*, Paris: Clancier-Guenaud, 1984.
4. In this article of 1935 ('The Manic Defence', Winnicott, 1975: 129–44), he contrasted 'fantasy' with 'reality'. It was only much later that he arrived at the term 'fantasying'.
5. 'Counter-transference' (1960) (Winnicott 1965: 158–65).
6. The Christmas cards, Clare Winnicott recounts were traditionally their work, which kept them up until two in the morning in the days before Christmas. Once, Clare Winnicott suggested that the drawing looked better left as it was in black and white, to which Winnicott replied, 'Yes, I know, but I like painting' and he went on to colour his Christmas card.

    Joyce Coles tells how in 1968 he was held up in New York, seriously ill; it was touch and go whether he would be able to go back with Clare Winnicott (in time for Christmas).

    'Realizing that he set great store by those Christmas cards, I wrote asking him to draw something and I would do the rest – the rest being to get the drawing made into a stencil for our duplicator, and then I used to "roll off" about 300 copies and fold them ready for signatures and post. . . . I managed to get these ready by the time he got home so that even in that year his many friends did get a hand-drawn Christmas card. . . . The painting was all done individually by hand on the black-and-white copies.'

(Letter, 19 July 1983)

7. 'Metapsychological and Clinical Aspects of Regression within the Psycho-Analytical Set-up' (Winnicott 1975: 278–94).
8. Winnicott (1971a: 65).
9. 'The Observation of Infants in a Set Situation' (Winnicott 1975: 52–69).
10. J. P. M. Tizard, speech delivered at Dr Winnicott's funeral, *International Journal of Psycho-Analysis*, 1971, 52: 227.
11. To the patient in *Holding and Interpretation*.
12. 'Hate in the Counter-transference' (Winnicott 1975: 194–203).
13. Preface to *La consultation thérapeutique*, the French edition of *Therapeutic Consultations in Child Psychiatry*.
14. Winnicott (1971a).
15. Winnicott (1971b).
16. Winnicott (1978: 184).
17. 'Primitive Emotional Development' (Winnicott 1975: 145–56).
18. The work of analysis with a psychotic involves the patient's body. As he recounts in 'Hate in the Counter-transference', he admitted that for a few days he was making mistakes in respect of each of his patients. 'The difficulty was in myself,' he writes, 'and it was partly personal but chiefly associated with a climax that I had reached in my relation to one particular psychotic (research) patient.' The difficulty cleared up when he had a 'healing' dream:

> 'In the first [phase] I was in the "gods" in a theatre and looking down on the people a long way below in the stalls. I felt severe anxiety as if I might lose a limb. This was associated with a feeling I have had at the top of the Eiffel Tower that if I put my hand over the edge it would fall off on to the ground below. This would be ordinary castration anxiety. In the next phase of the dream I was aware that the people in the stalls were watching a play and I was now related through them to what was going on on the stage. A new kind of anxiety now developed. What I knew was that I had no right side of my body at all. This was not a castration dream. It was a sense of not having that part of the body. . . . The second part of the dream . . . referred to my relation to the psychotic patient. . . . This right side of my body was the side related to this particular patient and was therefore affected by her need to deny absolutely even an imaginative relationship of our bodies. This denial was producing in me this psychotic type of anxiety, much less tolerable than ordinary castration anxiety.'

(Winnicott 1975: 197–98).

19. 'Fear of Breakdown', *International Review of Psycho-Analysis*, 1974, 1: 103–07.
20. Winnicott (1971a: 117).
21. Ibid., p. 55.

## Winnicott and Paradox

22. Cf. Keats: '. . . which Shakespeare possessed so enormously – I mean *Negative Capability*, that is when man is capable of being in uncertainties, mysteries, doubts, without any irritable reaching after fact and reason' (letter to George and Thomas Keats, 21 December 1817).

23. Winnicott (1971a: 55).

24. Organizers: Maya Cariel and Emmanuel Goldenberg. Observer: Jeannine Kalmanovitch. A group of six participants, made up of physicians, psychologists, and para-medics.

25. 'Mind and Its Relation to the Psyche-Soma' (Winnicott 1975: 243–54).

26. 'Overlapping Circles', article unpublished in English, published originally in French, translated by Claude Monod as 'Chevauchement de cercles', *L'Arc*, no. 69: 70–6.

27. Cf. Winnicott: 'The breathing may be associated sometimes with absorption, sometimes with evacuation . . . It manifests a continuity between inside and outside, that is, a failure in the defences' ('The First Year of Life', *The Family and Individual Development*, London: Tavistock, 1964).

28. J.-B. Pontalis, 'Le corps et le self', note p. 38.

29. Winnicott (1971b: 3).

30. A. Clancier, 'Le corps et ses images', in J. Guillaumin (ed.), *Corps et Création, Entre Lettres et Psychanalyse*, Lyon: Presses Universitaires de Lyon, 1980.

31. Winnicott (1971a: 103).

32. Thus absence is gradually constituted in Gabrielle's game.

33. Marion Milner, 'For Dr Winnicott Memorial Meeting 19 January 1972', London, British Institute of Psycho-Analysis.

34. On the interviews with trainee analysts held by D. W. Winnicott as a member of the Commission of Enquiry of the International Psycho-Analytical Association.

35. Taken by Arthur Coles, the husband of his secretary, Joyce, who kindly gave us permission to reproduce them.

36. Cf. Masud Khan, Preface to *La consultation thérapeutique*, (French translation of *Therapeutic Consultations*).

37. Cf. The case of David in 'The Manic Defence' (Winnicott 1975), in which he expects to be tired.

38. 'Aggression in Relation to Emotional Development' (Winnicott 1975: 204–18).

39. W. H. Gillespie, speech delivered at Dr Winnicott's funeral, published in *International Journal of Psycho-Analysis*, 1971, 52.

40. Cf. Winnicott (1971a).

41. According to Tizard, op. cit.

42. Gillespie, op. cit.

43. 'A Personal View of the Kleinian Contribution' (Winnicott 1975: 171–78).

44. 'Psychiatric Disorder in Terms of Infantile Maturational Processes' (Winnicott 1965: 230–41).

45. Winnicott (1965: 173).

46. Both James Strachey and Joan Riviere came from the same British Edwardian background: both belonged to the same circles in Cambridge, in particular the group of friends that met at Joan Riviere's uncle's house, a centre for activities of the Society for Psychical Research, which produced the only publication (apart from Janet's works) that dealt with abnormal psychology (according to James Strachey). Freud contributed to it in 1912.

    Strachey and Riviere came together after the war in their common interest in psychoanalysis in the Glossary Committee, which met at the house of Ernest Jones to decide on the translation of psychoanalytical terms.

47. Elsewhere ('Metapsychological and Clinical Aspects of Regression within the Psycho-Analytical Set-up', Winnicott 1975: 278–94), he writes:

    'The treatment and management of this case has called on everything that I possess as a human being, as a psycho-analyst, and as a paediatrician. I have had to make personal growth in the course of this treatment. . . . I have had to learn to examine my own technique whenever difficulties arose, and it has always turned out in the dozen or so resistance phases that the cause was in a counter-transference phenomenon that necessitated further self-analysis in the analyst.'

48. 'Counter-transference' (Winnicott 1965: 161).
49. C. Chiland, 'Winnicott au présent. Situation de Winnicott dans la psychiatrie et la psychanalyse contemporaines', *Psychanalyse à l'Université*, June 1980.
50. 'Communicating and Not Communicating' (Winnicott 1965: 179).
51. It is a training intended for professionals coming from very different backgrounds or for parents that is offered by the Winnicott Memorial Fund of the British Psycho-Analytical Society or The Squiggle Foundation – paradoxical manifestations if one remembers that, during Winnicott's lifetime, he remained without a school.
52. H. Sauguet, preface to *De la pédiatrie à la psychanalyse*.
53. Winnicott (1957).

# Chapter 6

1. R. Gaddini 'Reunion, Symbolization and Denial of Separation', *L'arc*, 1977, 69: 77–83.
2. M. Perron-Borelli, 'L'investissement de la signification', *Revue française de psychanalyse*, 1976, 40: 4. *Psychanalyse et langage*, pp. 681–92.
3. Winnicott (1975: 233).
4. Winnicott (1971a: 5).

5. Ibid., p. 6.
6. Ibid., p. 9.
7. Ibid., p. 18. 'String: A Technique of Communication' (1960) (Winnicott 1965: 153–57).
8. M. Soulé, 'Le mérycisme du nourrisson', paper read to the XXVIe Congrès des Psychoanalystes de langues romanes, *Revue française de Psychanalyse*, 1966, 30: 5–6, 735–43.
9. R. Gaddini and E. Gaddini (1959), 'Rumination in Infancy', in L. Jessner and E. Pavensted (eds), *Dynamic Psychopathology in Childhood*, New York: Grune & Stratton, 1959; and E. Gaddini, 'On Imitation', *International Journal of Psycho-Analysis*, 1969, 50: 478–84.
10. Cf. the case described by Winnicott in *Holding and Interpretation*.
11. The quotations in this section are all taken from Winnicott (1971a).
12. H. Searles, 'Counter-transference. A related subject', *Selected Papers*, New York: International University Press, 1979.
13. Joanna Field, (M. Milner), *On Not Being Able to Paint*, London: Heinemann, 1950.

# Conclusions

1. P. C. Racamier, 'Les paradoxes des schizophrènes', *Revue française de psychanalyse*, 1978, 42: 5–6, 865–71.
2. D. Anzieu, 'Le transfert paradoxal', *Nouvelle Revue de Psychanalyse*, 1975, 12: 49–72.
3. R. Roussillon, 'Du paradoxe incontenable au paradoxe contenu' (thesis), Lyon II, 1978.
4. R. Roussillon, 'Paradoxe et continuité chez Winnicott', *Bulletin de psychologie*, 1977, 34: 350.
5. Ibid.
6. Winnicott (1971a: xii).
7. Roussillon, 'Paradoxe et continuité'.
8. Ibid.
9. 'Psycho-Analysis and the Sense of Guilt' (Winnicott 1965: 16).
10. S. Freud, 'Some Character-types Met with in Psycho-Analytic Work', Standard Edition, vol. XIV, p. 311.
11. 'Fear of Breakdown', *International Review of Psycho-Analysis*, 1: 104.
12. Winnicott (1986, pp. 8–9). The remaining quotations in this section come from the same work, pp. 36–7.
13. Preface to *De la pédiatrie à la psychanalyse*, the French edition of *Through Paediatrics to Psycho-Analysis*.
14. 'Child-Analysis in the Latency Period' (Winnicott 1965: 115–23).
15. Introduction to Winnicott (1971b).
16. 'The Aims of Psycho-Analytical Treatment' (Winnicott 1965: 166–70).
17. Clare Winnicott, 'D.W.W.: A Reflection', in Simon A. Grolnick *et al.* (eds), *Between Reality and Fantasy*, London and New York: Jason

Aronson, 1978. The quotations in this and the following section are from this article.
18. Cf. the interviews at the back of this book.
19. A title from T. S. Eliot's 'Little Gidding' (*Four Quartets*).
20. Winnicott (1971a: 52).
21. Reproduced following p. 77.

## Alby's interview

1. Cf. case 1 in Winnicott (1971b). The mother in turn was able to express her feelings towards this child to whom she had passed on her own malformation. A more realistic attitude on the part of the mother, the child, and the medical team resulted from his interviews.
2. Winnicott addressed psychoanalysts on this question in his paper 'Hate in the Counter-transference' (Winnicott 1975: 194–203) and a conference organized by the medical section of the British Society of Psychology ('Counter-transference', Winnicott 1965: 158–65).
3. Clare Winnicott relates how when the young Donald once asked his father, who had a simple, religious faith, a question that might have involved them in a long argument, the father simply replied: 'Read the bible and what you find there will be the true answer for you.' ('D.W.W.: A Reflection', in Simon A. Grolnick *et al.* (eds), *Between Reality and Fantasy*, New York and London: Jason Aronson, 1978.)
4. Thus Winnicott dedicated his *Playing and Reality*, 'To my patients who have paid to teach me.'

## Kestemberg interview

1. The 'as if' personality was described by Helene Deutsch and is comparable with Winnicott's notion of the false self.
2. E. and J. Kestemberg, 'Contribution à la psychanalyse génétique', XXVIe Congrès des psychanalystes de langues romanes, *Revue française de psychanalyse*, 1966, 30: 45–6; E. Kestemberg, 'La relation fétichique à l'objet', *Revue française de psychanalyse*, 1978, 42: 2–3; and *Cahiers du centre de psychanalyse et de psychothérapie du 13e*, vol. 3, Paris, 1981.

# Name index

167

# Winnicott and Paradox

# Subject index

169

facilitating environment 8, 14–16; *see also* good-enough
faeces 85
falling 52
false self 20, 25, 51, 59–62, 66, 113, 137, 141, 148; *see also* self
fantasy 65, 130; and anxiety 19, 20; of omnipotence 20, 62, 87; oral 40; *see also* child and fantasy
fantasying 44, 88–9, 130
father 78, 117–18; death of 32; Oedipus complex 92, 95–7; support from 11, 16
fear: of breakdown 50–5, 66, 93, 94–5; of death 53–4; *see also* anxiety
'Fear of Breakdown' 50–4, 68, 94, 139
fetish 85, 130
Finland 106
'First Year of Life, The' 70
friendship 25
frustration 15–16, 47, 51
fusion 32

games *see* playing; squiggle
good-enough mother 11, 18–19, 43, 47–8, 51–2, 58–9, 62, 108, 110–11; *see also* facilitating
grief 20, 44
guilt: defence against *see* manic; emergence of 15, 19–20, 156; id-impulses and 33–4, 42; lack of 127–28; paradox of 93, 94; sense of 19, 94

hair-pulling, compulsive 86
handling 12; *see also* holding
hands 81; *see also* transitional object
hate: and love 40–2, 47, 78; *see also* aggression; depressive
'Hate in the Counter-transference' xiv, 67, 68, 165
hesitation 34–9, 66
holding xii–xiii, 9–12, 17, 29; interviewees on 107, 126, 136
*Holding and Interpretation* 48, 61, 67–8, 78, 88, 95–7, 153, 158
'hole' effect 19, 41, 60
hope 66; delinquency as sign of 56–7
hopelessness 57
Hôpital de jour du Parc Montsouris (CEREP) 105, 111

humour xiv, 22–3, 71
Humpty Dumpty analogy 14, 33
Hungary 108

I *see* integration; person; self
identification 16, 21
id-relationship/id-impulses 23–5, 26–7, 33–4, 42
illusion and disillusionment 29, 42–9, 62, 66, 87; breath and 67; independence, towards 46–9; interviewees on 109, 132, 142; weaning 44–6
imaginary companions 30–2
imitation 61
impingement 66
incommunicability 57, 62–3, 109
independence, towards 46–9; *see also* dependence; individual; person; self
individual *see* ego; environment-individual set-up; person, becoming; self
indwelling *see* inner
infancy 7–25, 117; parental care 9–14; *see also* holding; mother and infant; person, becoming
'Influencing and Being Influenced, On' 160
inhibition, intellectual 54
inner life and reality: denied *see* manic defence; incommunicable 57, 62–3; outer life and 19, 34–42, 58–9, 93, 102; and self, development of 30, 49; *see also* outer reality; self; skin
instincts 60
instinctual love 19
Institut E. Claparède 74
Institut de Psychanalyse 134
integration 15, 29–32, 33, 52–3, 66
intellectual: capacity *see* mind; inhibition 54
intermediate area 80; *see also* transitional area
internal environment *see* inner
International Association of Mental Health 133
International Congresses of Psychoanalysis *see* congresses
International Psychoanalytical Association xi, 137